·SOFT·
FURNISHINGS

SOFT FURNISHINGS

THE MOST COMPREHENSIVE AND UP-TO-DATE PRACTICAL
GUIDE TO MAKING CURTAINS, BLINDS COVERS, BED LINEN,
AND MANY OTHER HOME FURNISHING ITEMS

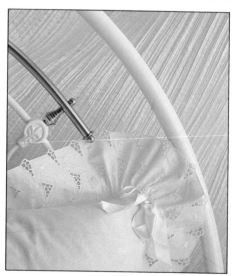

□ SARAH CAMPBELL AND HILARY MORE □

MAGNA BOOKS

This edition published 1989
by MAGNA BOOKS
MAGNA Road, Wigston
Leicester, LE8 2XH

Copyright © QED Publishing Ltd

First published in Great Britain in 1985
Published by Macdonald & Co (Publishers) Ltd
London & Sydney
A member of BPCC plc

British Library Cataloguing in Publication Data
More, Hilary
Soft furnishings.
1. Textile fabrics in interior decoration
I. Title
747'.9   NK2115.5.F3

ISBN 1 85422 053 5

This book was designed and produced by
QED Publishing Ltd
The Old Brewery, 6 Blundell Street
London N7 9BH

Editor: Sally Wood
Senior Editor: Tessa Rose
Editorial Director: Jim Miles
Designer: Hazel Edington
Art Editor: Nick Clark
Art Director: Alastair Campbell
Illustrators: Rob Shone, Steve Gardner, Vana Haggerty

Typeset by Leaper & Gard Ltd, Bristol,
and Text Filmsetters Ltd, Orpington
Colour origination by Universal Colour Scanning Ltd,
Hong Kong

Printed and bound in Hong Kong by Leefung-Asco Printers Ltd.

Special thanks to: Lucy Trench, Judy Martin
and Stonecastle Graphics, Tunbridge Wells

Contents
Foreword

Foreword

When my son was a very little child he so loved the bright patterns of my sister's sofa that he toddled along the length of it licking up the colours with his mouth: they were luscious to him. We must all be born with this ability to derive real and direct pleasure from look and touch; we need to – this is how we learn and grow. Many of us seem to lose the sure sense of knowing what we like and enjoying it; perhaps we have it squeezed out of us as we get older, and our strong feelings for what we want have to be constantly tempered by the reality of what we get.

I am lucky; for as long as I can remember I have been able to enjoy things with my eyes. My work as an inventor and painter of patterns gives me the chance to explore this love of colour, rhythm, texture and decoration fully and freely. I am in the favoured position of being able to work at and be in touch with the things that I love. Much of my work involves getting things wrong – that is, out of balance – and putting them right – that is, into harmony. In fact, we do this all the time; we are constantly evaluating the balances in our lives, and consciously or un-consciously shifting to try to keep comfortable. Mass-marketed, rationalized and mediocre 'solutions' in many areas of our lives can threaten our personal values and diminish our spontaneity and inventiveness.

We can challenge this; if we are aware, we can change things, and starting at a personal level we can seek ways to express ourselves positively, to redress the balance. A good place to start is at home. This is where we can be at ease, and openly explore our feelings; we can gain confidence in evaluating and choosing, and develop skills in making and inventing. It's a great feeling to clear away the debris of prejudiced and pre-determined 'taste', and to create something of your own that you love and respect. This is what this book is all about.

Sarah Campbell

Section One

Discovering your Style

The Nature of Fabrics

Fabric is an ancient commodity. The basic processes of its construction have changed little over the centuries. The skilful art of weaving cloth was developed very early in Egyptian culture, around 5,000 years ago; in areas where yarns were not spun, such as in the islands of the Pacific, cloth was beaten out from yielding barks and grasses; the Eskimos and American Indians, like other hunters, made supple materials by tanning the skins of animals; examples of knitted cloth, developed later than weaving, can be found from the early Coptic times in the third and fourth centuries. When these methods, and the processes of spinning, dyeing and printing were carried out by hand, the resulting fabrics were a personal record of individual skill and decision, based both on the intimate knowledge of available resources, and the social and practical end-uses of the product.

The primary uses of fabric must have been as protection – against the elements, both personally as clothing, and domestically as tents, shelters and wrappings; and against enemies, by the thickness of cloth, the unmistakable messages of war-dress, and the concealment of camouflage. This in turn led to the further protection of the wearer's identity and status – the chieftain's cloak, the widow's weeds. Another long-standing use of fabric has been as a convenient and flexible method of packaging and storing possessions. The portable homes of nomadic peoples illustrate how a particular way of life depends on and exploits the versatility of textiles. It is notable that even when living conditions are stark and disciplined, such as in the North African deserts, the fabrics, which are entirely functional, are highly coloured and intricately constructed and decorated: part of their function is to give visual pleasure and stimulation, as well as physical comfort, to both the user and the maker.

The pleasures of pattern-making and decoration have long been closely intertwined with responses to basic needs. This is apparent at all levels of society and wealth, from the marks applied directly to the body of a Kau tribesman to the most elaborate embellishments empowered by the wealth of princes. The huge tapestries once hung on the walls of Northern European great houses performed the simple task of minimizing draughts and interior cold, yet they were richly woven and embroidered, and replete with complex designs and images. Ceremonial and religious dress and furnishings have traditionally identified and confirmed status, and emphasized the import-

▼ A bedouin tent staked out in the North African desert. The black fabric structure houses a family group and its needs, providing protection against the extremes of temperature in this harsh environment. The woven goats hair material allows the breeze to blow through, but expands in the rain to give a watertight cover. When the time comes to move on, the tent and its contents are packed in a few woven bags to be carried to the next site.

▶ In contrast, the interior of this semi-permanent dwelling in Niger seems light and airy, with the patterned cotton walls making a decorative wind-break, and the cotton-covered woven frond roof giving protection from the hot sun. The exact form of the house is very flexible: another wall, or an internal division is easily made by unfolding a length of fabric and tying it to the posts.

ance of a specific environment and its accompanying rituals. Indeed, we in the modern West are constantly reminded of the image we are presenting by our own clothes and decorations.

These traditions are centuries old. In modern industrial societies, most people have become many times removed from contributing directly to the design and manufacture of fabrics. There are also many more complex ways of meeting basic requirements for protection, security and comfort, and for satisfying the urge to decorate and make our mark on our surroundings. But far from being relegated to a secondary role, fabrics have become more profuse and versatile, through the inventiveness applied to both their manufacture and their different applications.

In the space of a lifetime, the raw ingredients of fabrics and the resulting systems of their manufacture have undergone remarkable development and expansion. New synthetic and man-made fibres have increased the range in terms of the visual and tactile properties of the fabrics themselves, affecting possible end-use, price and availability. Over a longer period, since the development of powered looms and the invention of chemical dyes, a previously unforeseen array of colours and patterns has been devised through related technologies. Fabrics are produced in enormous quantity and with increasing complexity of design and construction. The wealth of materials now available for domestic use can seem both exciting and intimidating when it comes to making individual choices: our removal from the making of the cloth, and our bombardment with the 'made' can make understanding and relating to decorative fabrics a perplexing task.

NATURAL AND MAN-MADE FABRICS

Fabric ingredients fall into three major categories: natural, which are constructed from vegetable and animal sources such as cotton, flax, wool and silk; man-made, which are natural fibres re-generated and chemically treated; and synthetic, which are completely chemically derived. Natural fabrics are often preferred to synthetic materials for their appearance, feel and durability. Their very naturalness seems more sympathetic, and gives a sense of continuing traditions, and they have a life about them that has to be coaxed out of synthetics with special fabric conditioners. Chemical fibres were first developed in an effort to imitate the qualities of silk by a more economical means of production, and the notion that they are merely cheap substitutes has persisted, despite the many levels of quality and price covered by the products of this now large industry. Industrial production is less land and labour intensive than agricultural production, and the raw materials have been readily available – polyesters, for example, are petrochemically based. However, not all synthetic fibres are cheap, and many have been developed not as substitutes but to extend the range of fabric types. They are also used in fabric mixes – that is, in combination with natural fibres to contribute or supplement particular properties.

Materials as diverse as satin, corduroy or lace are made with 100 per cent cotton fibres; they can also be constructed entirely from man-made and synthetic yarns. Natural fabrics respond well to cleaning and care, having a basically resilient structure; synthetics easily attract surface dirt and need more frequent washing that can deaden the texture. The easy-care reputation attached to man-made fabrics derives from the fact that they generally resist shrinkage and creasing, and are less absorbent than natural cloths. The susceptibility of cotton to shrink or fade should be taken into account when making up large items that need regular washing, but various treatments are given to natural fabrics that modify their less convenient properties.

Colour is applied to fabrics by different processes of dyeing and printing, in both cases using colouring agents technically known as dyestuffs. Natural fabrics accept colour very well; in dyeing, the fibres can be saturated with colour to produce particularly resonant and full tones. The non-absorbency of man-made fibres presented problems in dyeing which were overcome by the development of special dyes that would take on such materials. The fact that different fibres have to be treated with different dyes introduces greater complexity and scope to the colouring of finished fabrics which are mixtures or blends of various ingredients.

Dyeing can be carried out at different stages of the manufacturing process. Wool and hairs, for example, may be dyed as fibres before they are spun. Fibre-dyeing allows for yarn to be spun in a combination of colours and textural qualities. Alternatively the yarn can be hand-dyed after spinning, and

colour mixtures made by twisting different yarns together. The third option is to dye the constructed goods, or grey-cloth; this is generally the cheapest method of applying colour. This does not mean that the fabric must be all one colour; because of the variations in acceptance of dyes, in a mixed fabric it is possible to dye each type of fibre separately by successive application of the appropriate dyestuff which can be of different hues. It may be necessary also to carry out dyeing in stages to bring all the fibres up to a single even colour.

Colour and pattern variations can also be developed from dyed fibres and yarns during the construction of the fabric – by weaving or knitting the colours together in particular configurations such as in tartans, tweeds, tapestries, jacquards and warp-dyed cloths. The nature of these patterns, though enormously variable, is ultimately dictated by the internal structure of the fabric. The various methods of fabric printing override this particular consideration, so there is an infinite number of design possibilities – given that a printed pattern is subject to the size of the printer's roller, screen, block or transfer, and therefore the repeat of the pattern has to be considered as an integral part of its structure. Printing introduces a different quality of colour; though printed colours penetrate the cloth to a greater or lesser degree depending on their type and application, their effect is of colour sitting on the surface rather than emerging from the body of the fabric as dyed colours do.

Mass-marketed fabrics are subject to a number of tests for different properties: resistance to abrasion, creasing, shrinkage or stretching; colour fastness under exposure to light, repeated washing and surface wear;

◀ A French version of a tented room. Here the bed is dressed traditionally in a style devised to offer both warmth and privacy in an age when central heating and private bedrooms were unheard of. Panels of fabric have also been stretched on the walls of the room in the manner of old tapestries. The pattern itself is based on a traditional Indian tree motif, and gives a light softness to a rather grand and lofty room.

▶ A rotary-screen printed fabric emerging from the rollers to be inspected and packed. The pattern, 'Côte d'Azur', has completed a long journey from the designer's paint-brushes, through the colour separating and screen cutting processes, to be printed, steamed, washed and finished ready for delivery as printed goods.

dimensional stability and the strength of individual fibres; draping qualities; the tendency of the surface to become picked or felted; the amount of 'give' in a fabric weave, and its ability to recover its shape. At this level the different qualities are assessed in highly technical terms and contexts. For a shopper, it means that information is available about the behaviour of a material and the care it will need, so it can be known whether it is designed to meet practical requirements.

LIVING WITH FABRICS

The choice of fabrics for personal use is relatively simple. Clothing meets a mood, or an individual preference or necessity; with our cultural codes it is possible to express our purpose, position and feelings within a particular situation – the little black dress 'reads' differently from the gold lamé trouser suit, the crisp linen costume from the tight jeans. We can change our clothes at will to suit day-long practicality or a special occasion or a change in the weather. Moreover, the fabrics used are essential to the effect – that black dress won't be made of tweed, the tight jeans must be denim. Choosing fabrics for soft furnishings may seem more taxing. They often require a substantial investment both of time and money, and the choice has to allow for as much versatility as a whole personal wardrobe and yet remain more or less permanent. They must respond to, accommodate and reflect different uses and moods, be seen under artificial and day light, act predictably and reliably on a given scale, correspond to the other permanent features in the home.

The choices made about furnishing fabrics can, however, be just as positive and personal as those affecting styles of clothing. People have a very direct physical relationship with soft furnishings. Quite literally, we are constantly in touch with them – sitting on a chair, relaxing on a sofa, nestling in cushions, sleeping among bed linen, drawing back the curtains. The colour, pattern, texture and overall feel of each item contributes to our comfort and pleasure on a day-to-day level. Equally, an inappropriate choice can detract from a real sense of being at home in our surroundings.

The pleasure of fabrics derives from the generous nature of the many different qualities they offer, single and collectively, in texture, form and colour. From the basic fibres – cotton, wool, linen, silk and synthetics – come materials of many different weights and textures: fine net, lawn or muslin; light, medium and heavy weaves which may be tight, smooth, slubbed or open; figured fabrics, and those with a nap or pile; light knits, dense tweeds. If you define fabrics in terms of their surface texture, they can group easily under these four headings: shiny, matt, textured and see-through. In the shiny category comes chintz, satin, cotton that has been mercerized, satinized or polished, ratine, sateen and Shantung, moiré and Indian silk, ramie and PVC. The matt fabrics include canvas, plain and patterned cotton, gingham, linen, hessian and union, dimity, sheeting, cretonne, baize and felt. Under

Fabric Directory

Fabrics can be divided into two groups: natural and man-made. Into the first category fall fabrics made from vegetable and animal materials: wool, silk and cotton. Man-made fabrics and materials produced by mixing chemicals with raw materials. Examples are: rayon, acrylic and PVC.

COTTON-BASED FABRICS

Cotton is made from the hairy, fibrous seeds of cotton plants. As a fabric it is hard-wearing, strong and absorbent – an ideal fabric for home furnishings. Problems of shrinkage and creasing can be solved by treating the fabric or by mixing it with man-made fibres to add easy-care properties.

Brocade: a fabric made up of areas of different weaves which form a raised pattern.

Buckram: This stiffened, coarse cotton is used for lining pelmets.

Calico: a cheap cotton of a medium weight that can also be printed.

Casement: a light, plain fabric used for curtains or for their linings.

Chintz: a glazed, medium weight cotton, usually printed with birds or flowers.

Crash: a coarse cotton with an irregular texture.

Damask: similar to brocade, this fabric is flatter with a soft, satin weave.

Gingham: a firm, light-weight cotton woven into checks. It is hard-wearing and fade-resistant.

Lace: an openwork fabric whose pattern is applied to a mesh background.

Lawn: a light, delicate fabric that can be woven into stripes.

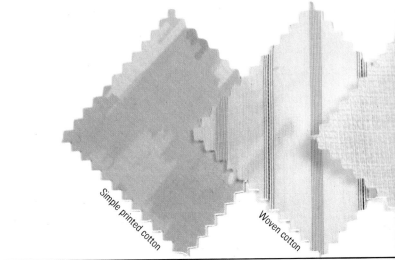

Simple printed cotton

Woven cotton

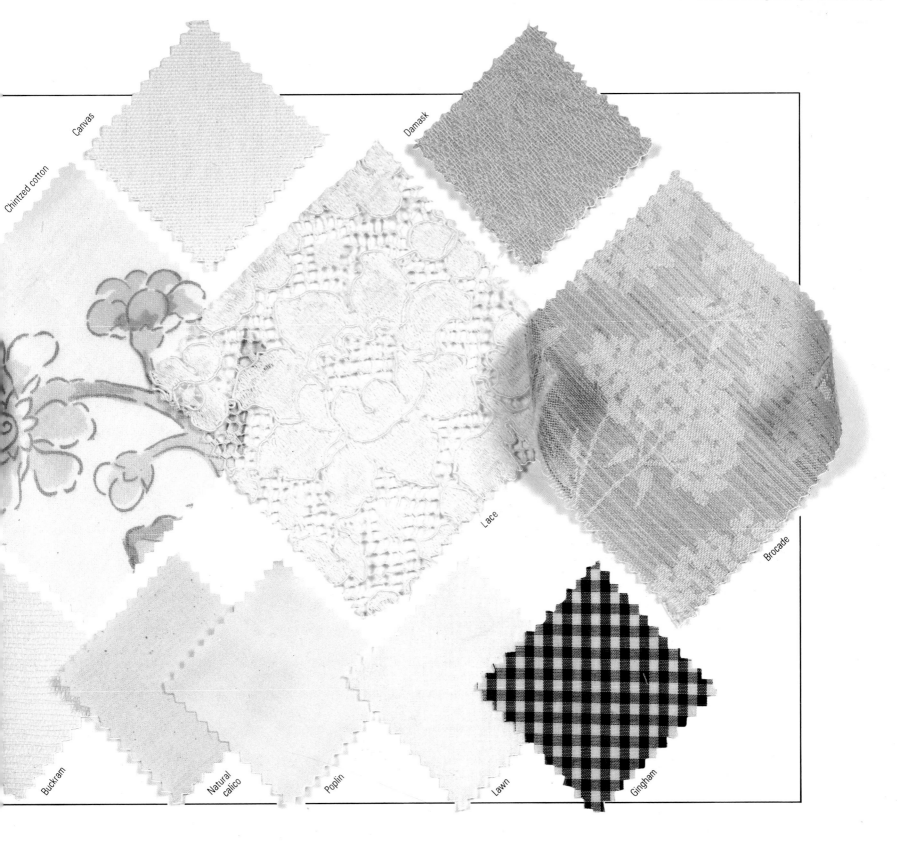

Canvas

Chintzed cotton

Damask

Lace

Brocade

Buckram

Natural calico

Poplin

Lawn

Gingham

Madras: a woven design fabric, often in a checked pattern, dyed with bright colours.

Poplin: a light-to-medium-weight plain, fine-rib fabric.

Sateen: a woven fabric that has a shiny smooth right side, with a matt wrong side.

Seersucker: a non-iron fabric made with puckered sections, usually printed in corresponding checks or stripes.

Sheeting: extra wide fabric, suitable for making curtains and wide-width blinds.

Velvet: a cut-pile fabric which stands away from the backing.

Velveteen: similar to velvet, but with a shorter pile.

Voile: light, open-textured fabric, suitable for sheer curtains.

OTHER VEGETABLE FIBRE FABRICS

Linen: an expensive, hard-wearing fibre which comes from the stems of the flax plant and is stronger and heavier than cotton. Linen can be woven smooth or in an uneven weave or slub. Linen is often mixed with man-made fibres to improve its qualities.

Cambric, chintz and **damask** can all be made in linen fibres.

Hemp: lighter in colour, with a coarser fibre than linen, this fabric is used to make hessian.

WOOL-BASED FABRICS

Wool comes from sheep, goats, camels and rabbits and is soft and absorbent with good insulating properties. It does not crease, but is often mixed with man-made fibres to improve its wearing qualities as well as making it cheaper to buy.

Boucle: the yarns of this fabric are treated to produce curls and loops.

Felt: a bonded, non-woven fabric that does not fray. It is easy to stitch without a right or wrong side. It is sold in wide widths to make it a cheap alternative fabric for curtains and blinds.

SILK-BASED FABRICS

Silk threads are spun from the cocoons of the silkworm. The fabric produced is soft and lightweight with good draping qualities. Next to nylon, silk is the strongest thread and can be woven or knitted into a fabric. But silk is also expensive, so imitation man-made fibres are often used.

Brocade: a heavy, ornate fabric, often woven with silver or gold threads.

Moire: this fabric is finished with a process that produces a wavy effect in the grain. That is why it is sometimes referred to as water silk.

Raw silk: this is the natural fibre spun together, making it coarser than other silks.

Satin: similar to cotton sateen.

Velvet: similar to cotton velvet.

MAN-MADE FIBRES

Acetate is made from treated cotton linters. After treating, the threads are twisted together to form the yarn. It is a cheap, soft and silky yarn that drapes well. Acetate is also resistant to moths and mildew, has easy-care qualities and will not shrink. Acetate is used to imitate silk for fabrics such as brocade and moire and is often mixed with silk and cotton.

Acrylic is light and soft with the bulky feel associated with wool. It is warm, strong and crease-resistant, but tends to pick up dirt quickly. Acrylic is often mixed with wool or cotton as in Dralon velvet for curtains.

Nylon is a completely synthetic fibre made from coal. It is strong, lightweight with easy-care properties. Nylon does not crease, is unaffected by moths and mildew. It washes well and dries quickly. White nylon can discolour easily, but can be revitalized. It is made up into many different fabrics, such as voile, lace and net, seersucker or satin. Cire is a nylon treated to make it waterproof – ideal for lining shower curtains.

Polyester is a versatile fabric that can imitate wool, silk, cotton or linen. It is hard-wearing and crease-resistant. Because of these qualities, polyester is often mixed with cotton to make easy-care sheeting. Most sheer fabrics for net curtains are made from polyester as it is not affected by strong sunlight.

PVC (Polyvinylchloride) is a non-porous, synthetic, coated fabric with a knitted or plain-woven cotton base. It comes in various weights, but can be difficult to sew. Its qualities make it a good everyday kitchen table cloth.

Seersucker

Voile

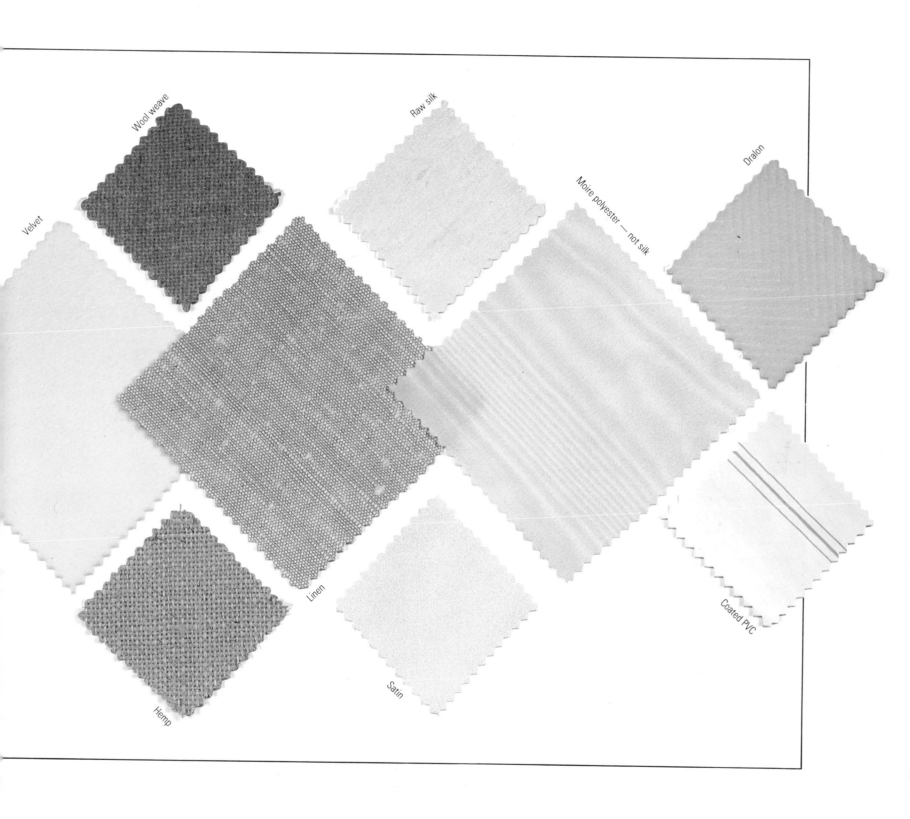

Wool weave

Raw silk

Dralon

Moire polyester — not silk

Velvet

Linen

Hemp

Satin

Coated PVC

textured and pile fabrics come velvet, chenille, Jacquard weaves, Ottoman moquette and damask, brocade and brocatelle, taffeta, towelling and seersucker, corduroy and burlap. Among the see-throughs are muslins (both dotted and butter), cotton and synthetic lace, parachute silk, holland and gauze, nets, sheers and burnt-out fabrics. Within each group there are categories of quality dependent on the exact weight and nature of the yarns used, and the density at which it is constructed. To these innate properties are added an infinite range of possible colours. The complexity progresses with woven and printed patterns in a variety of scale and distribution – spots, stripes and checks; florals of all shapes and sizes; tight geometrics and painted abstracts; even cartoons, stories, pictures and graffiti.

So, when you walk into a well-stocked fabric department, the possibilities are inviting but also bewildering. If you start with a definite idea of the particular materials you want, you may be sidetracked by a striking design or colour completely different from your imagined choice. If you wander round hoping for inspiration, it can be difficult to identify what it is you really like, and what will do the job, in terms of shaping up as curtains or upholstery. Besides, the fabrics are bound in books, or massed together in bales or rolls, or presented as the store's display designers see fit. This particular context does not correspond to the conditions and environment in which you will use and appreciate them.

It is obviously important, then, to identify clearly what it is you wish to do with the fabrics, and to assess your response to the qualities of the different materials that you value and might like to use. There are many elements involved in your choice, with strands of habit, instinct and feelings about yourself intertwining with expectation and social pressures; in this state of indecision you may fall prey to the dead hand of fashion – that is, the hand that markets derivative styles of decoration which promise much but can never really deliver because the application is so often inappropriate. Small suburban windows filled with frilled, ruched and ballooned bloomer-like blinds are a typically ridiculous example of 'hot-air' styling.

One offered solution to the problem of knowing what to choose has been the packaging and presenting of ever-expanding ranges of completely co-ordinating fabrics, which cross-classify with other products such as wallpaper, china, paint and accessories to produce a 'total look'. A style is established, culled often from a cultural or literary source, and the basic colours and pattern motifs are styled to form common elements which unremittingly link each fabric to its fellows, and guarantee a room scheme with neither accident nor incident. These packages are marketed across a variety of price points and decorator styles – 'country' florals, 'romantic' chintzes, 'city' geometrics, even *Dynasty*'s telly-glamour. They can resolve a crisis of confidence about mixing and matching, but more cynically they can also create one. If the stylist, the advertisers and the store buyers all imply that success lies in having blue roses from egg-cup to three-piece suite it may be hard to disagree. If you go for the whole look you could be landed with a predictable and lifeless camouflage that bears no relation to your own life.

Side by side with this planned co-ordination has been a fashion for layering and combining different fabrics to produce a richness of colour, pattern and texture. This could be achieved by using part of a co-ordinated range as a basis to which you can add and supplement from wider sources, or invented by a random and instinctive mixing of disparate prints and weaves. In short, take one step further than the given solution and you begin to create an environment that is pleasing, personal and lively.

The confidence to make positive choices comes partly from understanding the physical elements that influence your requirements and direct your decision. These are identifiable as the spaces in which you live: their shape, height, scale, and the objects already within them; the way the light enters or fills the rooms, its colour and strength at different times of day; the practicalities of your way of life – who uses the rooms, when, what for, and how often; the personal preferences you have for colours, styles and atmosphere; the innate properties of the fabrics and how they can be used to their best advantage. You need to make spaces that will nourish you, allowing you to re-charge and encouraging you to progress.

▼ This room successfully combines many different patterns, textures and fibres, drawing together fabrics that are woven, knitted, printed, crocheted and patched. The fabrics sit happily, both with each other and with the different materials around them — wood, brick, tiles, mirror — and reflect the work of several different cultures and traditions. They have been collected with a real love of textiles, and this feeling unites them in an easy harmony which is neither claustrophobic nor contrived. The strong stripes of the woven rugs and crocheted blanket are a good foil or 'container' for the less formed floral patterns, and make a pleasing reference to the ceiling beams. Similarly, the diamond patches on the cushions relate to the diagonally set floor tiles.

▲ Though of different qualities, the soft furnishings and rug in this sitting room are all woven from the same raw material, cotton yarn. The excitement comes from the positive use of two active patterns within a calm environment. The fabrics are printed with very different designs, which are united by their similar lively spirits and their vigorous use of fresh bright colours. They relate both to the soft old terracotta and pine at the window, and the shiny new black plastic or lacquer of the table; the natural cotton rug gives a cool serenity to the scene, allowing the patterns to dance about freely. Such strong designs tend to elicit a direct response; this is in contrast to the patterned fabrics in the picture on the left, which take time to make themselves known.

Space and Light

Light defines space, form and colour; these are the basic elements of composition in two- and three-dimensional design. In planning the look of an area or room it may be helpful to regard it as a walk-in painting, in which a variety of shapes, colours, tones, patterns and textures will be assembled and balanced within a given space. The interior architecture acts as a framework within which your eye and your imagination can wander, elaborating different details of the room or inventing an overall impression.

The shape and scale of the room are given quantities, as is the amount of light it receives. It is easy to identify the dimensions and atmosphere; for example, the room is large and airy, with high ceilings and expansive windows, or small and intense with a narrow beam of light from one angle. It may be L-shaped and better lit in one area than another, or irregular with quirky features such as a sloping ceiling and deep recesses. Strange shapes, awkward corners and poor natural light often occur in house conversions, where small rooms have been carved out of larger ones. You will need time to identify how you feel about these characteristics. Stand back and use your hand as a spy-glass to frame each area as you come to it to help you to assess its merits and possibilities. Linger in each corner of the room, and concentrate on it from all angles. Should the fabrics be used in ways to exaggerate or co-operate with the room's idiosyncracies, or be planned to counter and disguise the less pleasing elements?

A spacious, well-lit room is an open canvas. It will take plenty of colour, bold patterns, variety. Large windows can be surrounded with strong fresh hues that dance in the light, or hung with soft translucent fabrics – lace, net, muslin – that need light filtering through to show off their talents. If you have a small, gloomy room you may struggle to lighten it up by using pale cool colours to open out the space; but why not be hung for a sheep as for a lamb, and turn its small darkness into a tiny lush-coloured den full of softness and visual texture?

It is important too, to realize the relationship between different spaces and anticipate visual links and contrasts as you move between rooms, or see one area framed against another. This applies for both colour and style: if you were to connect a predominantly blue room with a mainly yellow one, would you find the contrast alarming or exciting? Would you feel comfortable moving from traditional floral patterns into bright primaries without a neutral zone in between? A white room might look twice as effective if you enter it from a deep-coloured corridor, but how will you feel as you leave and the process is reversed? The gentle progression between like elements or the surprising display of differences can both have their own continuity and vitality: it is for you to decide.

In choosing colours for soft furnishings, you can afford to be ambitious. Fabrics are not harsh and immutable – they are fluid, subtle, changeable; when used, they are given both form and movement. All sorts of different effects are perceived in the play of light and shade. These come from the modelling of a form as the light falls across it; from the way light is absorbed or reflected at the surface of the material; from the internal structure of the fabric, and whether the colour permeates the whole texture, is mixed and blended within the weave, or printed across it. You may call your chair green, but look and see how many colours it really is.

Fabrics have intrinsic properties in relation to light. They are opaque, absorbing light or reflecting it from a matt, figured or shiny surface; or they are translucent, by virtue of a lightweight or open structure. The different ways a fabric will be seen depends upon the changing light within the room and the form and position of the fabric itself. The effect of a pattern seen as the light strikes it on the horizontal plane of a table or a bed, for example, will be different from that experienced when the light is absorbed in the folds and layers of fabric hung vertically as curtains. Heavily textured fabrics have one aspect when evenly lit close to a window; nubbly or honeycomb weaves, and details such as gathers and pleats take on a more sculptured effect when the light is angled across them.

Translucent fabrics give of their best when clear light is filtering through, but bear in mind that they will also be seen against grey, weak daylight, and as lit from inside by artificial light. Lace fabrics, those with colour detail or a material that folds and billows such as muslin, make the most of light coming from different directions. A fine fabric with a degree of opacity looks good with light falling on as well as through it. Heavier fabrics used for curtains or lampshades will also be seen both lit on the surface and with light coming from behind at different times of day.

There are appropriate ways of using the weight and texture of different materials to combine function with decorative effect. There are no hard and fast rules about this; it is largely a matter of common sense, and developing an instinct for the right time to take a risk. A well-shaped solid sofa covered in satin of a vivid colour has immensely satisfying qualities, both to the eye and the hand. But if it is a case of re-covering an old sofa, a shiny fabric will accentuate mounds and hollows, and a better choice would be a thick, matt or patterned fabric which absorbs light and has sufficient weight of its own to contain the underlying form. More texture and fullness are good means of disguise for flaws in shape and proportion. A straight drop of pleated fabric at a bedroom window, for example, will draw attention to a sloping floor or bumpy wall, where a softer treatment will deal more kindly with eccentric geometry. Colours too have their capacity for disguise – dark rich colours can soak up imperfections where light tones might be too brittle and resistant.

◀ A large, cool, modern interior is given a surprising element of humour by the visual joke of the two people printed sitting on the sofa! The bright colours focus the eye, and the flowing figurative print is in clever contrast to the rather uncompromising grid lines on floor, ceiling and furniture. A modern house, where space and light are often distributed in unconventional ways, has room for these decorative adventures.

▶ This bedroom has a simple and romantic atmosphere. The light, softly filtered through a translucent curtain, makes a filmy rainbow at the window, and then sparkles off the shiny brass of the bedstead. The soft white fabric on the cushions and the bed itself gently reflect the different tones, and serve to emphasize the very direct relationship between colour and light.

Colour and Pattern

Colour lives in light: it is not a static entity and its qualities are so affected by its neighbours that almost the only rule about colour is that there is none. Colours can come forward or recede, extend the space or fill it up. They can seem to have weight or substance – those that are commonly described as rich or deep- or they can be airy and elusive like the blues and greys of the sky. At the same time, colours provide atmosphere. They can be warm or cool, calm or excitable, inviting or austere; their effect depends on how they are used. I sometimes catch a distant glimpse of a bus: the small rectangle of red against the large expanse of green creates a buzz of visual excitement, and its contrast accentuates the space. But if all the walls of a room were painted that same red the space would seem filled, and the occupant enveloped. Where reds and purples seem to be substantial, soft greys and greens tend to be relaxing, keeping their distance and making space to breathe. Clear colours such as limes, yellows, pinks, oranges and fresh blues and greens have a zingy effect, suggesting energy and activity, particularly when they are seen against white or soft cream, or with their contrasting colour. I have recognized a friend by her glowing orange hair sparkling against a blue-green hillside 2 miles in the distance. Use the same clear colours with black and they will have a different look, a sort of electric glamour as opposed to a sunny vigour. Because of its powerful light-absorption and disagreeable associations, black may be seen as oppressive or mournful; but it can be exploited to provide strong contrasts and sharp delineation. And a highly polished black chintz can elegantly outshine the brightest colour.

No colour is seen in isolation. Colours are always perceived in relation to each other, as harmonies and contrasts, mutually enlivening or subtly inter-locked. It is worth taking time to look at how colour works. Josef Albers, among several Bauhaus artists, did many paintings exploring the effect one colour has upon another, and it would be worth borrowing a book of his work from the library. Of course you can do your own experiments. Buy or paint some different coloured paper squares; choose one colour, let's say red, as the subject of your investigations, and pin the pieces on the wall in pairs – red next to green, then red next to yellow, and again the same red next to blue, and then next to another red and so on, as many as you like. Take a good look at them all, and you will begin to see that the same red reads differently as it is influenced and swayed by its adjacent colour. Try it with other colours, or in different textures or shapes, pinning different coloured triangles inside the subject-coloured squares, for example, or small pieces inside much larger ones, and watch what amazing tricks colour can perform!

You can carry your experiments further by changing the paint colours

◄ The same red appears different when juxtaposed with different colours. Here the red is dominated by yellow, sharpened by the blue, dampened by green and thrust forward by the black border.

▲ The effect of placing different colours next to each other in a room can be seen here. Although all the primary colours are present here, and the result is somewhat strident, the jazzy effect is melded into a harmonious whole by the repeated angular abstract signature.

themselves. By adding squeezes of different colours you can evaluate the degree of change and determine what you need to make your red more vibrantly orange, more softly pink, more deeply purple or more dusty; how to take the edge off its brashness, perhaps, and relate it more subtly to its companions. The more you increase your sensitivity to colour, the greater the pleasure you derive from it.

Colours are evocative, and there are complex levels of association. Some derive from the natural order – the wholesome and camouflaging safety of earthy browns and ochres; the bright colours and strong contrasts of reds, yellows and blacks that are used as display and danger signals by plants and animals; the properties of life and growth suggested by clear and vigorous greens; the mysterious richness and luxury evoked by jades, rubies, sapphires, turquoises. There are also cultural associations, illustrated by the naming of certain colours: sunshine yellow, lollipop pink, airforce blue, pillarbox red, battleship grey. Most important when it comes to living with colours are personal associations and preferences. These may come from having lived with a particular colour before and having good memories attached, or they may have to do with objects and ideas you associate with a colour – the warm naturalness of terracotta, a sense of luxuriant smoothness in an ivory or pearly white. Try writing down the names of some colours and the associations that they trigger off.

The effects of colours also relate to the shapes in which they appear. Pink stripes or pink roses make different statements about the nature of that colour, and the style of the design itself evokes particular and longstanding associations and responses. Traditional florals may be thought of as girlish, pretty or countrified, while geometrics could suggest coolness, sophistication, urbanity. Colours can be used to play up such associations or to cut across them – by inserting a hard glamorous red into a softly rounded flower, or sending up the austerity of hard-edged geometry by painting it in candy colours.

Pattern, like colour, operates actively in a given space. Mankind seems always to have been a mark-maker. Our use of pattern and decoration has a longer history than our use of cloth; the need for us to express ourselves in this way is deep. Pattern so often re-creates and explains the shapes, forms and natural geometry of the living world that it is reasonable to conclude that pattern-makers and users have a need to define and make sense of the complexities of our relationship with our surroundings, and re-invent them again and again. The language of pattern takes on all sorts of extra meanings – magical, social and cultural symbols emerge, and the original references are lost. Certain motifs have been used for many centuries and in several different cultures; the paisley shape, for example, has now become for us a key to a particular Oriental luxury and richness in design. Other symbols, like the swastika, have had their meanings changed by sinister applications and are no longer acceptable.

Pattern has long been an intrinsic part of the language of soft furnishings. At one end of the scale the simple re-iterative rhythm of a small one-colour motif repeated on a plain ground can give a sense of well-being and comfort;

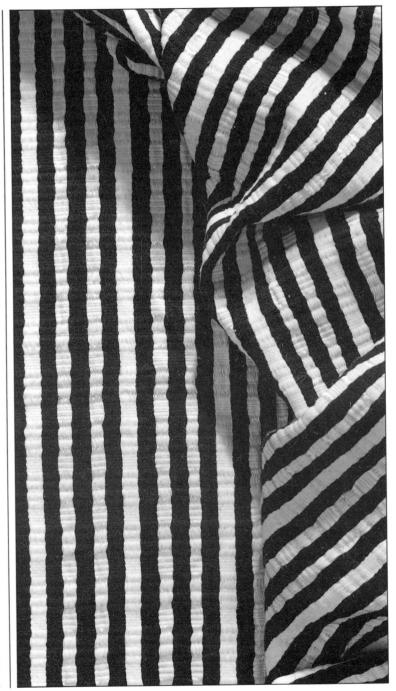

◀ Here the classic stripe is given a home on an armchair designed by Alvar Aalto in 1936, and in production again today. The stripe is a perfect partner for the graphic shapes of the trolley and the chair. The image is clear but not cold, and it makes easy reference to the basic geometry of line and circle, and the basic materials of wood and fabric. The lack of applied colour emphasizes the purity of line and form.

◀ A stripe is a stripe is a stripe . . .? The beauty of this one (woven by Helene Jungnicke in about 1922) is that it shows how much life there can be in a very simple and familiar pattern if it is made in a vivacious and original way. The quality of the yarn, the textured weave, the careful balance of black to white, all make this a particularly pleasing and exciting fabric, both when seen flat-on and in rippling folds.

▶ In contrast, this mass of patterned fabric (Collier Campbell, 1983) derives its charm and excitement from the eclectic use of colour and design. The patterns themselves have their origins in the woven tradition of carpets and paisleys, but being painted designs they can throw off the structural constraints of a weave and move freely across the cloth, juxtaposing areas of flat colour with areas of complicated and intricate pattern. Both these pictures illustrate how well the appropriate use of patterned fabric can complement a room and perfect an image.

25

at the other end, a large pattern painted with many colours and an ingenious and sophisticated repeat can present a challenge, demanding and deserving space and attention. Between these two extremes lie many alternatives in scale, subject matter, style and colour.

Lots of patterns tumbled together or loosely layered draw in the space and give it visual texture. Large patterns can be used with small, dense with open, printed with woven to make the collection interesting and varied. Areas of pattern placed in an orderly way among plain-coloured expanses can divide and separate the space, creating well-defined focal points, and adding drama to the room. Pattern can also be used to emphasize and define form: a bold design extravagantly custom-cut and fitted to enhance the shape of a particular chair, say, can give a witty and surprising style to an everyday object. The emphasis of the pattern is a vital factor in its effect. Vertical stripes will tend to heighten a window drop, while used horizontally they will draw it out widthways. Certain patterns have a pronounced direction, such as a diagonal,

that must be accommodated or exploited; others have a busy all-over effect that creates movement within the piece but offers no spatial illusionism.

In formal terms, pattern introduces a great deal more complexity to fabric treatments. The colours have been deliberately chosen and distributed within the design, but where a patterned fabric is gathered, pleated or draped, the internal shapes are broken up and put into different relationships. The size of a pattern repeat on a length of fabric has a logical scale which can be wasted if it is cut or extended inappropriately. A large figurative design can be awkwardly snapped off by the planes of an upholstered chair; small delicate motifs may get lost at a vast expanse of window. Designs require as careful consideration by their users as by their painters. Fabric pattern-books and samples cannot always show the full extent of a single repeat, so it is important to see all the shapes and colours in a design in order to match it to a particular function, and to know that it will make sense among neighbouring objects and images.

◀ Almost every surface in this room is patterned or decorated; harmony is achieved by the careful balance of colour and pattern. The naive roses and fronds on the table cloth relate in their hand-painted style to both the rag rug and the embroidered silk hanging in the background. The bamboo sofa introduces another hand-made, garden-y element, and is covered in a print which marries well with the stripes of the rug and the colours of the printed and stitched flowers. The green-grey softness of the furnishings is given another dimension by the informal arrangement of fresh leaves and branches.

◄ The unusual shape of this impressive chair has been emphasized by the white piping used as an outline on the plain black upholstery. By setting it between the scarlet rectangle of wall, and the large red dot of the rug, the chair is given a particularly sculptural presence. This quality would have been disguised had the chair been covered in a busy all-over pattern.

▲ Here a bold geometric pattern is given an unexpected soft look by being printed in gentle landscape colours. This does not detract from the strength of the design, but allows it to sit well in the feminine setting of a pretty bedroom. The shiny, figured damask tablecloth makes a good companion, adding another element in design and surface texture while making space for the colours of the print to breathe and expand. The combination is restful, but not cloying.

Making Choices

There is clearly a range of practical considerations to be taken into account when you buy fabrics for soft furnishings. They must be suitable for the job in hand and be able to withstand normal wear and tear for a useful period. You may be operating within a limited budget, or ready to splash out on something special. If you have a particular scheme in mind, examine it critically to make sure you can live with it through changing moods and requirements. If you consider indulging a fantasy – a pure white room, a tented interior – do you want it open to children, animals, guests or business associates, or do you have enough space to separate it from the main living areas? Think about all the people who use the spaces, what each room is for, and at what times of day it is most used.

You know from the experience of buying clothes or ordering a meal that making the wrong choice, for whatever reason, can leave you feeling miserable and deprived. It follows that an appropriate and positive one replenishes and satisfies. To make a good and enjoyable choice you need to feel good about yourself, and be able to recognize your wants and discover how to realize them. Often decisions made instinctively on a love-at-first-sight basis are the right ones; they can indicate your very strong, possibly unconscious feelings – for colour, shape, texture, light. Don't be deflected from your target, your hunch, by the "I shouldn't have that" syndrome. If you have privately long wanted something apparently outrageous or unconventional, allow yourself to see why and what exactly you think it would be doing for you. It may need to be modified slightly for the sake of practicality, but hang on to the essence. On the other hand, if you need time to come to a sure decision, take it. Let your imagination wander through the possibilities and what-ifs, so that your ultimate choice can be made positively for the product, not out of a sense of defeated confusion.

A useful practical approach is to collect odd lengths of the fabrics you have a feeling for. These can be thrown over a chair, draped at a window, or made up into a simple cushion. Manufacturers sometimes lend sample lengths that you can try out, or you may find likeable remnants and sale bargains. This gives you the opportunity to live with an idea in a temporary form, so that you can get a sense of how the patterns look as you come through the door, what the textures and colours do under daylight and at night, how a fabric feels when you finger it or lean against it, what it does for other aspects of the room, its furnishings and your other possessions. This is particularly helpful if you are choosing a fabric in a very different style or colour from your established preferences.

It is ultimately worthwhile not to skimp on quality or quantity in fabrics for furnishings. This does not necessarily mean paying a high price. A range of

◀ One of the keys to deciding on a 'look' for a room is being able to explore any fantasies you might have about it. These two bedrooms, for instance, take this to extremes. This bed is dressed like a bride; the lace canopy hangs like a veil, filtering the light and modestly protects the bed in virginal white. The lilies are a symbol of purity; the look is unsullied.

◀ These two sitting areas again show extreme and opposite ideas in their decoration. Here the room has become a church dedicated to the art of 'kitsch' — the symmetrical arrangement of the table and lights is reminiscent of an altar, at which the fake fur sofa seems like a sacrificial offering.

▲ In this bedroom (designed by John Wright) the feeling is more like that of a sophisticated bordello. Plush carpets, lurex drapes, a fat pink quilt and the scarlet decor offer the sleeper quite another image. Both rooms make strong, if opposing, statements about bedroom fantasies.

▼ This conservatory on the other hand, seems devoted to the cause of nature and naturalness. The furniture itself, covered in a floral print, is almost lost among the florabunda, and the desired illusion of an inside/outside garden is successfully maintained.

▶ Quick-change experiments with colour: here the basic ingredients are an old wooden chest, a mottled yellow wall, a bed and a cushion. On the chest are some favourite items linked by colour or subject-matter. The little postcard of Van Gogh's bedroom makes one yellow and blue image, the familiar globe another. The feeling of an island set in an ocean is reiterated in the stitched canvas painting (by Stephenie Bergman) tacked to the wall, and again in the predominantly yellow cushion set on the turquoise bed. Both these printed fabrics were bought in London street markets and have African and Caribbean connections. Under the turquoise batik is a colourful cotton dhurrie; on the floor is an Afghan rug and an embroidered Indian numdah. The whole has moved outwards from the particular, restating the theme of yellow on blue, blue on yellow. This type of decoration can be quickly changed. The blue theme has now been exchanged for a hotter colour look. The dhurrie has been tacked to the wall, and the bed covered in a hand-appliquéd felt blanket. The cushion now has a shiny magenta chintz print, and the hot reds and pinks are carried through to the woven basket on the wall and the bright flowers in a Chinese enamel bowl. The merry tassles and bright colours of a Mexican shawl make a fine foil for the elegant grey cat!

relatively inexpensive cottons – from muslin to heavy canvas – can fulfil all the different functions, from softly-gathered window nets to hardwearing upholstery. You may need to adjust your ideas to accommodate a limited budget: instead of packaging the whole room from floor to ceiling in one go, treat it simply with a minimum of plain fabric and create an exciting focus by covering only the bed or sofa with something colourful, exciting, expensive. Take your time: start with one or two items in this way and build gradually to the complete effect over a longer period. Think too, how details can enrich the atmosphere – plump cushions, ribbon trims, corded pipings.

An aspect of the lovely versatility of fabrics that should not be overlooked is the many different uses of already-made items. You can change the nature of a room very quickly with light throwover covers for a chair, sofa or bed – a large shawl could do the job, or a pretty tablecloth, a woven blanket or simply a length of another interesting fabric. A dhurrie or similar soft rug does not have to live on the floor: it can be tucked over the sofa seat, flung over the back or hung on the wall behind, to give a different style to upholstery. Hand-made items offer a particular charm and vitality; you may have inherited some old lace or a Kashmir shawl, or have some embroidery, crewel, patchwork or quilting that has a personal history. These sorts of things are not hard to come by in your travels, in auction rooms, jumble sales or specialist and ethnic shops. Alternatively, you could decide to spend a lot of money on a one-off handmade item by a living weaver or designer. Fabrics of all kinds

offer many ways of adding to the quality and pleasure of an interior, often for little effort or expense.

Whether you have many ideas or none at all, it can be a problem to narrow things down, to make actual choices. The elements of good design are a curious mixture of proven effects and personal inventiveness. The environment in which you live is fundamental to your well-being, and there is a natural anxiety about getting it 'wrong'. Successful soft furnishings are those which have the right visual appeal and physical comfort to suit *your* taste, not those dictated by manufacturers, marketing agents and advertisers, and it makes sense to start with easily definable preferences and work outwards from there.

One key to your choices will be found in the other objects that you choose for decoration, stimulus and pleasure. If you habitually feel comfortable in plain, dark clothes, for example, would you be uneasy spending a lot of time among floral fabrics, or might you enjoy expressing that side of your nature in your home and not on your person? You collect things about you that indicate the different qualities you find agreeable, that make you smile – china, plants, pictures, seashells, toys, glasswear, books, boxes, baskets … all of which have varying colours, forms and textures. Study the things you like. Take some and play with them. Group them together in different ways: like with unlike, smooth with rough, or all the things of a similar colour, or all the patterned things, for instance. By getting to know them, the more abstract properties that form the links and contrasts can emerge as a model that you can translate into design with fabrics.

Pictures – paintings, photographs and prints – are a useful source of reference. They offer considered relationships of colour, pattern, tone and texture balanced within a strict framework to create a particular mood or message. As with baking a cake, the balance of the ingredients is paramount yet delicate: pictures can give you a strong feel for a composition or colour theme. This may come directly from the subject matter: a painting of a Dutch interior, for example, with its deep shadows, stillness and glowing light, or of Matisse's richly decorative salon; or a detail of a shelf with a still life, or a vase of flowers by a window; or a landscape which gives a wholly different sense of space, light and colour. It may be a matter of picking up the impressions of colours arranged in specific proportions in an abstract painting, or a feeling for the relationships of line and mass in a design. You may respond to the graphic drama of a Japanese print, or the patterned minutiae of an Indian illustration. Try to see these works in the flesh, the size they really are. Post-cards, bought from art galleries or stationers can offer conveniently portable reference: these small pictures can evoke an immediate response and bear a lot of looking at. You cannot live in a picture, of course – a painting is a sort of two-dimensional confidence trick – but by letting yourself be open to these compositions you can develop an independent view of their individual components and overall influence. This can be related to your own surroundings and will give you clues about collecting colours and fabrics about you that will connect in similar ways, and work for you.

Hopefully, the feelings you have about your home and the points of view that you want it to express and contain can develop through an expanding intimacy with colour, form and fabric. I cannot dictate decorator styles but it might be helpful to look at some different photographs that illustrate possible directions you could take.

◀ Here a bold Indian wall-hanging dominates the room, and gives an Oriental flavour to the furnishings. The ochre, black and cream shades of the painting have been used again in the fabrics on the bed, and the tiger stripes are echoed on the batik cushions. The creamy walls and window blind help to accentuate and relate the two areas of pattern and colour.

◀ This little collection is primarily of painted wooden objects, using strong colours and plenty of black. These look good shown off against creamy canvas and silk, which gives them a very luxurious feel. They relate well to the dramatic printed fabrics using black as their main theme with sparkles of scarlet, gold, jade and magenta to give life and light. It's fun to devise ways of using colour and fabrics to extend and enhance the feelings sparked off by a few likeable objects brought together.

▼ In contrast this group of objects, some everyday, some special, are linked by their soft neutral self-colours. The shiny silver dish and mother-of-pearl shells stand happily with the earthenware jug and basketful of wood-shavings. It is easy to make connections between the homely pottery and the natural canvas, or the wavy white shell and the creamy rippling silk. The printed fabrics in the background use fluid, spacious designs to reflect the harmony of neutral colours and natural materials.

Maximum

'Enough – or too much!' William Blake's philosophy is exemplified in this type of interior decoration. One of the feelings encouraged by such an expansive display is that there will always be new and delightful details to be discovered within it.

The Indian canopies around this bed make a rich room within a room, and give the luxurious and rarified feel of ancient embroideries. In fact the design is hand-printed, and this gives it a soft and sympathetic air which, although bright, is not garish. Within this decorated sanctum the deep colours and soft texture of the bed-quilt look warmly inviting. Outside the tent are other fabrics and carpets with yet more designs applied to them. But the effect is not overwhelming: getting to and from the bed becomes a marvellous progression through layers of varying light and pattern.

The unexpected and the non-sequitor abound in this highly decorated sitting room. Here things are not what they seem – tulips of glass and papier-mâché fruits, china frogs and wooden men, prints that look like weaves and a marquetry tablecloth inlaid on a wooden table. These illusions are housed within a framework of printed fabrics which share a common colour look of quite bright primaries. Each print uses a different combination or dominant element – yellow at the window, for instance, but not on the sofa. All the objects and patterns make reference to each other and are strongly linked.

▶ For details of swatches, see p.160

Minimum

The everyday comfort normally associated with fabric use is here understood from quite a different viewpoint. This is the art of 'less is more', of gaining greatest effect from the least components, and requires a disciplined and single-minded approach: it's hard not to let books pile up in the corner, or to prop post-cards against the window-frame. Such rigorous tidiness must require capacious cupboards for any house-hold clutter! The fabrics used are chosen with absolute authority for a specific and controlled effect. This single futon mattress has a simplicity which will attract the pure in spirit. It makes an obvious reference to the Japanese culture, which might seem here to be more ascetic than comfor-table. The fabrics themselves are very simple and traditional – a white satin for the pillow and a deep navy cotton for the mattress, enlivened by the white tags of the buttoning. All the action is concentrated here on the floor; it is accentuated by the height of this European room.

The enormous chairs in this sitting room look impressively sturdy and substantial. Their glossy bodies com-plement the wall of cloudy grey steel, and the glistening ceiling con-tinues this shimmering effect as it reflects the light from the windows. Both these pictures show a very pre-cise use of fabric, which allows for a complete appreciation of each ele-ment within the room. It does not make for cosiness, but for a rather awe-inspiring interior architecture.

▶ For details of swatches, see p.160

Harmony

The word harmony suggests a confluence of similar elements working together to make a pleasing and integrated whole. Contained in this is the idea of progression and movement between each different facet or strand of the composition. These rosy curtains are gently gathered to give a generous but not over-powering picture of traditional prettiness. The deep pink of their lining hints at the solid pink fabric of the bed valance, which in turn sets off the simple white bedcover with its fine lines of pink embroidery. On the table the feeling of delicate freshly-laundered cotton is echoed and expanded by the lacy cloths, and the whole room is cleverly drawn together by the grey-green carpet, which has the colour of soft lichen or willow leaves.

The stripy woven look of the Provençal print on these garden sofas works in harmony with the basketwork of their frames.

An adventurous showroom displays a group of fabrics whose colours were designed to work together, encouraging the eye to travel from pattern to pattern without being jarred by the changes.

▶ For details of swatches, see p.160

Contrast

An exciting decorative look can be achieved by the juxtaposition of clearly contrasting elements. This can be done simply by choosing 'opposite' colours which buzz off each other when put together – red and green, blue and orange or, as here, yellow and black. The contrast is underlined by the different uses to which the colours are put: the yellow occurs in the soft and natural shapes of the sofas and flowers; the black is used as a strict outline in the angular furniture and light. The other colours and materials in the room do not interfere with this arrangement, so that the nature of the yellow as a dancing, elusive colour is exaggerated by the static black.

Other contrasts can be made: for instance by putting together two different types of design – very floral with very geometric, say, or different types of fabrics such as a smooth silk and a rough weave. One can also make a conscious decision to exaggerate the differences between the nature of the fabric and its architectural surroundings: a simple bed is made more of by being placed against a huge expanse of brick wall, while elsewhere a very angular corner shows off a lush, colourful hand-painted sheeting design. The aim of the contrast is to bring out the individual quality of each element.

▶ For details of swatches, see p.160

Primary

The primary colours, which strictly speaking are red, blue and yellow, are often associated with the most simple elements in design, as they are shown to be the basics from which all other colours derive. They have become a natural choice for children's and young people's spaces. This tin toy collection is a good example of the use of bright colours to attract children – and their pocket money!

Clearly these toys are no longer for kids only, and neither are the primary colours of the sitting-room in which they live. The kaleidoscope of colour in the cupboard is contained by the natural pine, and then reflected back by the areas of flat, bright primaries in the room itself. The square blue and yellow cushions on the scarlet sofa take on an air of being toys or building blocks themselves. There is no need for any more pattern than that of the painted toys, and it is interesting that though very bright, these large expanses of different simple colours can be restorative in their uncomplicated clarity.

▶ For details of swatches, see p.160

Warm

Colour can give warmth to a room, making it a welcoming and comforting environment. This small dark room has been given great spirit and cosiness by the use of traditional furnishings in a palette of rich reds and blues. The busy patterns and textures of the Oriental rugs are contained and offset by the plain walls painted in a lush crimson. The solid chair is made lively by using mixed fabrics in the upholstery; the cream cushions bring light relief to the redness. The depth of the colours is enhanced by the furniture made of deep polished woods, and the eastern feel of the carpets is echoed in the collection of Turkish-looking ceramics. The room is given a further dimension, and any hotness is refreshed by the reflection in the large rectangular mirror of a light hallway beyond.

Warm colours do not always have to be red. Here it is the rich quality of colour that glows and gives warmth: the generous depth of the turquoise of the wallpaper is accentuated by the bright flicks of colour on it, which are then continued and extended by the range of hues in the curtain – jade, turquoise, and crimson mixing with dusty rose and deep vermilion. The bright yellow funnel of the light adds a surprising contrast. It is often the intensity of colour that gives warmth.

▶ For details of swatches, see p.160

Cool

Giving a room a cool, calm airy feel can enhance its natural light and space and make a relaxing pool of quiet sophistication. An effective way to achieve this is to keep colour to a minimum, and concentrate on delicate, subtle neutrals. There is no need for such a room to be stark or devoid of interest: this sitting-room, for example, has different printed patterns on the walls, blinds and sofas. They are united by their colour look, which ranges from off-white through creams, sands, soft peaches and greys to the most gentle browns. The windows have simple flat blinds: gathered curtains or festoons would have made unnecessary clutter. The subtle patterning of the wool carpet is made by sculpturing the pile. The other objects in the room offer a variety of textures and visual interest through the materials themselves – chrome, leather, marble, glass, wood, ceramic. There is plenty to appreciate in this cool room, but nothing invades the space clamouring for individual attention. In this calm, elegant bedroom the simple sheet design is reminiscent of the tonality of damask, and is given a witty liveliness by the slim ultra-marine lines and bindings.

▶ For details of swatches, see p.160

Section Two
Creating your Style

Windows

Whether stark roller blinds or soft festoons of fabric, window dressings set the style of a room. They enhance or obscure the shape of the window and lend light their own particular quality. During the day, they're the world's proscenium. At night, they meld the mood.

▶ An abundance of sheer, ruched fabric makes an extravagant covering for a narrow window. Catch the corners to the frame and fasten at the middle with a large floppy bow allowing the extra fabric to spread round the base.

Shapes and styles

The windows in any house are rarely uniform in size and shape – it would be a dreary sight confronting the outside viewer if they were. To a large extent, architectural styles dictate the way in which a window is treated.

Whatever its shape or size, a window is a decorative as well as practical feature of any room, with a major role to play in the overall scheme. The actual shape or position of the window may be impossible to change, but the way it is dressed can dramatically improve its appearance and set the mood of the whole room. If strategically integrated into the design, the window will become important in its own right, providing a splendid focal point in even the dullest interior.

Bay and bow windows Square or angled bays and the rounded bow-type window (*fig 1*) should be treated as a single unit if the curtains are to look their best. Flexible nylon or aluminium track, which can be moulded to follow the line of the window area, is convenient and can be extended at either side to avoid fabric bunching. For a lavish effect, the track can be mounted above the bay, and the curtains hung from ceiling to floor; but it may be necessary to keep the curtains sill-length to clear a window seat or radiator below.

Casement windows Generally opening outwards and placed in groups of two, three or four, casement windows (*fig 2*) are common in many older houses. If they are deep-set, curtains can be mounted inside the frame on invisible track so as not to restrict the opening mechanism. If floor-length curtains are preferred, they must be hung outside the frame, along the length of the group of windows.

Sash windows Georgian-style sash windows (*fig 3*) are elegant and attractive so the window dressing should enhance, not conceal these features. If hung on invisible track or a decorative pole mounted outside and well above the frame, curtains will not conceal the natural beauty of the window frame when drawn back during the day. Alternatively, swags or valances may be considered suitable to offset this type of window.

Horizontal windows Often found in modern houses, these windows (*fig 4*) tend to be uninteresting, if not actually ugly, and need some clever dressing to lift them out of the ordinary. Careful positioning of the track or pole can help to correct unsatisfactory proportions and the curtains should be generous and, preferably, full-length. However, if the windows are deep-set with wide sills, short curtains hanging inside the window frame (either hung on a track placed on the inset of the window or hung on expanding wire) are more suitable. For the high, clerestory-type of window, where conventional curtains are unsuitable, sheer materials, which can be kept closed on track fixed above and below the frame, are a possible solution.

Picture windows Typical of modern houses, where there is a large expanse of glass giving access to a garden or patio, picture windows (*fig*

▶ An overall use of pastels gives a fresh and bright atmosphere to this living room. The distinctive deep pencil pleat headings meet across the curtain tops. And to add to the feeling of height, the curtains are caught back way above the middle. Plain nets hang behind the curtains to give privacy, and to cut down on excessive sunlight.

1 Bay or bow windows.

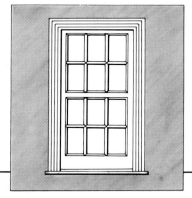

2 Casement windows.

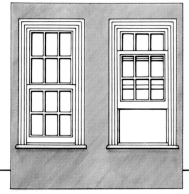

3 Georgian-style sash windows.

4 Horizontal windows.

5 Picture windows.

6 Pairs of windows.

7 French windows.

8 Corner windows.

9 Portholes.

10 Dormer windows.

5) or patio doors demand a generous approach with both curtain fabric and lining. The curtains should be full-length and adequately lined to provide insulation against heat loss. Where there are separate doors and windows with wall space between, three curtains of varying sizes may look better than two symmetrical ones hanging at either end.

Pairs of windows Whether of the same shape and size or irregular, closely linked windows (*fig 6*) should be treated together. Floor-length curtains may be preferable. Suspended from a single track or pole across the top of both windows, they can be drawn back evenly at either side or drawn to the centre as well.

PROBLEM WINDOWS

The choice of curtain for standard windows usually depends simply on the style and mood of the room, but awkwardly shaped, misplaced, disproportionate or irregular windows call for special treatments. Whatever the problem, windows are there to provide light, so curtains should not be hung where they will shut the incoming light out.

French windows Where these are made up of both doors and windows, they should be treated as one single unit, with a pair of curtains covering the entire glazed area. If there is only one working door, there is a danger of too much fabric restricting its opening so, in this situation, a single curtain, pinned well back to one side with a decorative tie-back, is more convenient. They are more usually made up of two doors (*fig 7*) and a pair of curtains can be employed.

Corner windows Where two windows meet at a corner, leaving minimal space in between (*fig 8*), a single pair of curtains is sufficient to cover both windows. The tracks should be mounted above each frame, the inside edges butting together so the curtains meet when drawn. If poles are preferred, they must be in wood so that the ends can be mitred for a neat butting join. The curtains then open outwards from the corner, hanging close to the outside edge of each window frame when drawn back.

Portholes Generally, round, port-hole windows (*fig 9*) look better uncluttered by curtains. But if covering them is necessary for privacy, curtain them with a covering that has narrow casings. Make a straight curtain and thread the casings at top and bottom with covered wire. Hold in place round top and base of frame, as well as at intervals in between. Make small buttonholes in the casings to accommodate the hooks that hold the wire. Then tie the curtain in the centre with a decorative bow.

Dormer windows With tiny, deep-set dormer windows (*fig 10*), it is necessary to make use of the adjoining walls to accommodate curtains of any fullness. Flexible track, bent into a U-shape to fit into the recess, enables the curtains to be drawn back to the side walls to let in maximum daylight.

Slanted top Where the window top is slanted to fit under a sloping roof (*fig 11*), it will depend on the position of the window in relation to the ceiling as to where the window coverings should be placed. If the window is directly under the ceiling the curtain track will look best fixed along a straight horizontal line of the window, even if it means leaving the top skylight portion of the window uncovered. Alternatively, if the whole window must be covered, put up a ceiling-mounted track. If there is a good space between the ceiling and the window top, mount the curtain track straight above the window so the curtains will cover the complete area, and, when drawn will disguise the shape of the window underneath, simply by hiding it.

Arched windows Any treatment for beautiful windows like these (*fig 12*) must enhance rather than obscure their visual appeal. Choose an extra-long track or, preferably, a traditional pole secured well above the arch allowing the curtains to be drawn clear of the window. If the window is not overlooked, a shaped valance fixed permanently in place around the top of the arch may complement the arched window's attractive and unusual shape.

Skylights Treat skylight windows (*fig 13*) in the same way as pivoting windows covered below. Make up a self-contained curtain and fasten to the window frame with a cased top and base so that the covering will open and close at the same time as the window.

Pivoting windows Conventional curtains are unsuitable for windows which open on a pivot mechanism (*fig 14*), such as sloping attic-windows and skylights. Instead, the curtains should be made to fit the frame and be fixed to it on expanding wire or rods at top and bottom so that they open along with the window.

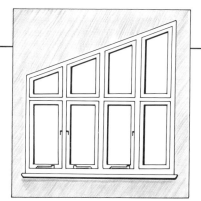

11 Slanted top windows.

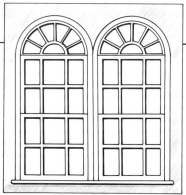

12 Arched windows.

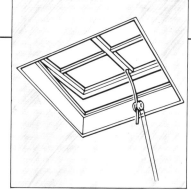

13 Skylight windows.

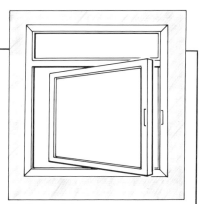

14 Pivoting windows.

▶ This is a very novel way of dressing a window — simple yet immediate. Although not to everyone's taste as a permanent fixture, it does allow you to live with a fabric for a while and to experiment with it before you commit yourself to one style.

Curtains

Curtains are often the natural choice for window dressing, both for the variety of colour, texture and style that they offer and for their practical advantages. They can: provide a screen for privacy or against a grim view; completely obscure light or filter it attractively; enhance the unusual features of one window or improve the dull appearance of another; visually transform the proportions of an odd-shaped room and improve the outward appearance of the most unprepossessing exterior; and, for the energy-conscious, well-lined curtains are an extremely effective means of insulation – keeping the warmth in, and the draughts out.

Before deciding on the precise effect you want to achieve, it is important to get down to basics, for even the most lavish curtains will not disguise a window in poor condition. Deal with any defects first, by replacing cracked glass or putty, repairing broken sashes and catches, and giving careful attention to the wooden framework. Where there is a build-up of old paint, strip it down to the bare wood, fill holes and cracks and sand the surface smooth before repainting; take time to apply primer, undercoat and at least two top coats of gloss paint, which will give a good, hard-wearing finish worthy of new curtains.

Decide how your curtains are to be hung and examine the condition of the existing track. Unless it runs smoothly, old track should be replaced to avoid undue wear and tear on curtain edges. Choose a modern, cord-operated system instead. Check that it will withstand the weight of heavier fabrics and increase its length if you want curtains well drawn away from the window for extra light. Consider how it will look when exposed and choose one which will blend in unobtrusively or can be painted to match the surrounding wall.

Alternatively, look at the wide range of poles which are meant to be seen – in brass, mahogany, natural or painted wood with matching rings and fancy finials.

There are many criteria, both aesthetic and practical, to consider when choosing the most appropriate curtains and a number of factors may influence the choice. The curtains should reflect and enhance the decorative style of the room, as well as fulfilling any practical requirements. An elegant town house, for example, will have large windows which dominate a whole wall and demand lavish dressing with luxurious folds of fabric and decorative headings; but this grand approach would be wrong for small cottage-style windows which need a simple uncluttered treatment, scaled down to suit an altogether different environment.

Before any decisions are made about the final effect to be created, the style of the room in which the new curtains will hang should be carefully considered.

Traditional interiors, with large rooms, high ceilings and large windows, may call for classical treatment in keeping with their period style. The curtains should be as grand as the setting, falling in lavish folds to the floor in luxury fabrics, such as velvet or brocade, or striking traditional chintzes. For the real 'stately home' treatment, those headings which make use of fabric – pelmets, valances or elaborate swags and tails – will have a suitably elegant air and, where the window is very tall, will help to reduce its overall height and minimize the void above.

If you want to create a nostalgic, romantic mood, the fabrics should be delicate prints or sheers, such as lace or voile, which filter daylight into a room to give a soft, feminine atmosphere. The curtains may be edged prettily with frills or braid and hung from Victorian-style rods in brass or dark mahogany.

If you live in a sophisticated town house, the curtains are likely to be formal in style, achieving impact through interesting texture or a smart, well-ordered pattern. Trimmings should be limited to a plain border, of bright webbing for example, if colour contrast is needed.

The country look in interior design may either evolve naturally or be deliberately created to modify an urban environment. Essential features are simple, functional furniture in natural wood, plain and patterned walls, and small windows dressed in a cottage style. The curtains should be simple, with track extending at each side to prevent small windows being dwarfed by too much fabric; and the fabric itself should be of a gentle and unsophisticated design.

If flamboyance is what you seek, try some extravagant oriental effects. Furnishing fabrics come in a wide range of lush designs on dark backgrounds reflecting the rich colours of lacquered furniture. Although the headings and trimmings should be kept simple for the most dramatic impact, the fabrics should be mixed and incorporated throughout the room to suggest an oriental opulance. Alternatively, a cooler oriental look can be suggested by a pale, monochrome room enlivened by splashes of stronger colour from simple striped and patterned fabric.

Window dressing for a modern interior usually calls for a controlled, almost masculine, approach to complement the deliberately restrained style. Simple geometric designs or textured fabrics and tailored styles make the strongest statement in a room where everything is straight and clean.

PATTERN, SCALE AND PROPORTION

Few rooms in any house are in proportion - they can be too small, too dark, too high or too low - but most proportional problems are surmountable, usually by exploiting the effects of colour and scale, in which the curtains can be a vital factor.

In small, low rooms where the ceiling seems oppressive, pale, unified colours will suggest a sense of space, especially if used with low-level furniture. It may be subtle, and effective, actually to match the curtains to the wall, whether plain or patterned. With the opposite problem - tall rooms with high ceilings that give an impression of coldness - strong, dark colours with bold patterned curtains may create visual interest and warmth. If, however, the airy formality of the room is attractive, it should be emphasised by cool, unobtrusive fabrics.

In rooms with sloping ceilings or odd-shaped walls and windows, plain fabrics, or those with small regular patterns, will deflect attention from these awkward angles. More drastic measures can be taken by curtaining walls, windows and doors in one sweep - an easy feat with modern flexible curtain track.

If the rooms are dark and sunless, light, flowery fabrics can introduce a summery atmosphere. On the other hand, if the atmosphere is too bright and glaring, it can be toned down with darker, richer patterns.

Fashion holds sway among curtains, too, and styles now range from simple, understated expanses of fabric, suitable for a modernist interior, to the elaborate adornments that create a period look or suggest a little fantasy. Here one can have swags and tails, looped elegantly over poles and bosses to cascade down the sides of the curtains; pelmets which tend to be structured and architectural in effect and may alter the proportions of the room; or pretty gathered valances which convey a romantic, feminine air.

Tie-backs may have a purely practical function: to hold back the curtains and allow light into the room, or they may be an integral part of the styling of the curtains, emphasising a formal, masculine design, or sweeping lavish curtains up into voluptuous folds. They can be made of fabric - matching or complementary, plain or shaped, padded and trimmed - or heavy cord, and should be designed to complement the curtains.

FABRICS

When choosing fabric for curtains, it is a good idea to take home large (50 cm) samples of fabric and to consider them carefully in the correct setting and light before making any final, and expensive, decisions. Then, when purchasing the full amount of fabric, you should check it for flaws as a mistake in the weave or pattern could mean the loss of a complete curtain drop.

Check that your chosen fabric has the qualities you need: will it wash well? be shrink resistant? will sunlight destroy its bright hues? Manu-

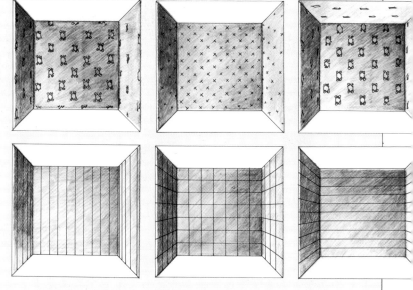

▶ The proportional faults of a room can be altered with the clever use of patterns.
1. Mix a plain ceiling with large prints to help to keep the height.
2. Small prints will give the impression of space when used in small rooms.
3. Using a large pattern on all walls and ceilings will make the room seem smaller.
4. Vertical stripes on all walls will make the ceiling seem higher.
5. Geometric patterns on all walls will give a feeling of space.
6. Horizontal stripes will make the room seem wider.

◄ Your choice of colour and pattern will help to emphasize or alter the dimensions of a room. The options of pattern matching and colour coordinating are endless, but you will have to introduce a few ground rules of your own in order to achieve the effect you desire. Ginghams, stripes and florals are perennial favourites and are perhaps the most common patterns used in the home today.

▲ These floor-length curtains in a floral print design look effective matched with the sofa covers. The simple top casings are threaded onto curtain poles and the centre edges are attractively finished with a band of toning fabric. The slightly longer length sweeps the floor helping to create a feeling of height in the room.

▶ Stylish triple-pleat heading adds to the opulence of these long-line curtains. Hung from an elegant brass pole with decorative finials that echo the ceiling mouldings, the curtains are drawn together at the top. They are swept across the windows and are held back with matching shaped tie-backs. When unhooked, the curtains will fall together neatly.

facturer's label or salesperson should be able to answer these questions.

If the fabric has a large pattern it will not only add to the overall cost, as allowances must be made for pattern matching, but it may also cause problems in the cutting out if the pattern is not correctly aligned with the straight of grain. This should be checked before purchase.

The lining and interlining should be bought at the same time as the curtain fabric, along with a suitably large amount of thread.

LININGS

These help curtains to hang better, cut out light and noise, provide added insulation against draughts, and reduce wear on the curtain fabric. Linings can be permanent or detachable. The latter are fixed to the curtains with hooks from a separate heading tape. Detachable linings make the curtains easier to handle by reducing the bulk when removed for laundering.

There are two types of lining tape: one is a pocketed tape that splits in half enclosing the raw top edge of the lining. The second tape is made in the usual way, but the loops that hold the hooks run along the top edge. In each case the curtain hooks loop through the lining heading tape first and then through the curtain heading tape, ready for hanging on the track. The simplest method of fixing the lining to a curtain is to 'bag out' the fabric with the lining, by stitching them together at the side edges, then treating the hem edges separately. But, for a really professional finish, lockstitch the lining

into position and then handstitch the side and base hems together.

Lining fabric is a tightly woven 100-per cent cotton fabric made in the same widths as curtain fabric, 120 cm wide (you can also get buff and white lining 137 cm wide) and in a range of colours. Plain buff-coloured lining is the cheapest, but you will achieve a better colour-coordinated look by matching the lining either to the fabric or to the paintwork around the window.

There is also a range of special linings. You can choose a lining that is coated on one side with particles of aluminium to help to retain the room heat or, to keep out the light, a black-out lining can be purchased.

Do not skimp when buying lining fabric; both loose and locked-in linings should be as full as the main curtains. Also aim for the best quality, otherwise you will find that the lining will wear out before the curtain fabric.

Interlinings A layer of interlining between the curtain fabric and the lining will ensure that your curtains hang beautifully and wear well. Interlining also provides an effective method of insulation.

It is available in a variety of thicknesses and 120 cm in width, the most common types of interlining are domette and bump. Interlining is not washable, so interlined curtains will need to be dry cleaned.

Widths of interlining are overlapped and stitched together with herringbone stitch. If the interlining is very thick, the stitching should be worked from both sides of the fabric to effect a good join. Interlining is locked to the wrong side of the curtain fabric and then treated as one fabric with the curtaining.

ESSENTIAL EQUIPMENT

When making curtains it is important to have a large flat surface to work on. A large table is preferable to the floor, but if you must work on the floor, make sure that it is clean and that you do not cut or mark the floor.

For measuring, you will need a steel retractable rule for your window and track, and a tape measure and metre stick for the fabric.

Use tailors' chalk or marking pen to mark the fabric, but if using a pen, test the colour on a spare piece of fabric first in case the marks can be seen on the right side of the fabric.

You will need a large pair of cutting-out scissors and a small pair of general sewing scissors. A sewing machine is a boon, although curtains can be made by hand.

Use extra long steel pins when pinning heavyweight fabrics together; and a strong medium-size needle for hand-sewing. And for pressing, use a wide ironing board and a clean iron and pressing cloth.

TRACKS AND POLES

Tracks There is a large variety of curtain tracks on the market. Most are now made of plastic, so they are cheap to buy, quiet to use and usually pliable enough to fit round the tightest bay windows.

As there is such a bewildering array of tracks, it is sensible to go and see the ranges on display before making any choice. Some manufacturers provide helpful booklets and leaflets

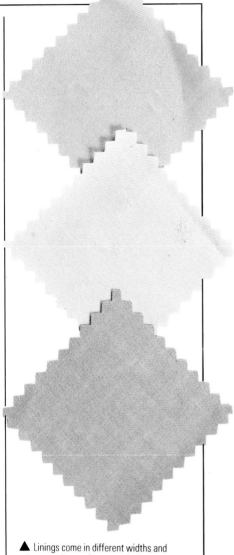

▲ Linings come in different widths and colours, and range from standard types (top and centre) to expensive aluminium-backed fabrics (above) through which light will not penetrate. The choice is yours.

showing how and where the tracks can be used. There is a wide variety of styles and finishes – metal or plastic, plain, painted or papered – to match the style of the room and the design of the curtains.

Each track comes packaged with fittings for securing to the wall or ceiling, end stops and runners. In some cases the runners also incorporate hooks.

Extras for curtain tracks include pulling cord systems to open and close the curtains, preventing wear on their centre edges, brackets to bring the track away from the wall to clear a heavy architrave, and overlap arms for a good closure in the centre. There are also valance tracks that can be clipped onto the main curtain

track so as to carry the valance in front of the curtains. Check that the track will support the curtains once they have been made – a considerable weight if the fabric is heavy.

Poles As with tracks, there is a good selection of poles, from traditional brass to natural wood, which can be polished, painted or stained to match the décor. They come in a range of lengths and diameters, and are sold complete with extra fitments such as curtain rings of the correct size with screw eyes for holding the hooks, brackets for fixing to the wall and finials to decorate the pole ends. Ready-corded poles, with rounded fronts that conceal an inner track system, are also available.

When curtains are hung from a

pole, the highest pocket in the heading tape should be used so that the curtain tops hang just below the pole, exposing rather than concealing it.

How to fix curtain tracks and poles Tracks and poles are usually placed between 5 cm and 10 cm from the top of the window frame, extending between 15 cm and 40 cm at each side of the window, depending on the size of the frame and the thickness of the curtain when pulled back. All tracks and poles can easily be cut to the correct length, so they should be bought one size larger than the required length.

Tracks and poles can also be suspended from the ceiling, or poles can be inserted into a window recess.

HEADING TAPES

Commercial heading tapes are strips of tough, durable fabric, available by the metre, which are stitched across the top of curtains. They are pocketed to contain the hooks that anchor the curtain to the track, and they also contain cords running through them which, when pulled up, form the decorative heading at the top of the curtain.

The heading tape influences the look of the curtain, so it is important to choose a tape that will produce the right heading, and merge with the décor and, above all, suit the fabric.

▶ Here the crisp tab heading mirrors the modern style of the room's décor. They are simple to make and do not require a heading tape. The loops hang from the curtain pole straight across the window top and the curtains are held back with stencilled fabric tie-backs.

▶▶ A small window can be given a sophisticated look with a beautiful glazed cotton chintz — and a matching circular tablecloth adds to the effect. The smart triple-pleated heading can be hand-stitched and made to overlap by the addition of a plain toning frill. Piped and frilled tie-backs contain the curtains' fullness.

Different heading tapes gather up varying amounts of fabric; simple gathered headings are more economical in fabric, the more elaborate ones use more fabric.

Random gathers Standard or cluster-pleat tape is used for this style and it gives a shallow, informal heading which is attractive for simple curtains, especially those in small windows, and for unlined curtains. For these, an allowance of 2.5 cm should be made above the heading to conceal the track. This heading is used, too, in more elaborate curtains, where a pelmet will conceal the plain top. It is the most economical choice of heading as it uses only one-and-a-half to twice the track length of fabric. Random gathering displays patterned fabric to advantage, but it is not suitable for heavyweight fabrics.

Pencil pleats The heading tape forms stiff, regular, closely-packed pleats and, as one might expect, uses a lot of fabric – two to three times the track length – to look effective. The tape usually has two or three pockets to enable the hooks to be placed in different positions to suit the type of track, and a deeper version of this heading is available for floor-length curtains.

Triple pleats These have a more formal appearance as the fabric is disciplined into three straight or fanned pleats with a wide, flat section between each group. The heading tape for pinch pleats is a simple and stylish heading which suits a plain, textured fabric, possibly hanging from a pole and rings. It needs twice the track-length of fabric and is available in different widths.

Cartridge pleats This heading consists of single 'goblet' pleats, which alternate with flat sections of fabric. It is best used with thick, lined curtains and the pleats can be padded with cotton wadding or tissue paper to maintain their plump shape. A button trim at each pleat adds to the sumptuous effect. Two to two-and-a-half times the track length of fabric will be needed with this tape.

Other tapes There is a number of decorative heading tapes in a variety of designs, such as smocked and tudor-style, which look particularly effective on sheer or fine cotton fabrics. They require twice the track length of fabric.

Net tapes are fine and lightweight so as to look transparent when stitched to sheer fabric. They need twice the track length of fabric.

Lining tapes are adapted to use with detachable linings: the tape splits around the top of the lining. Then one hook holds both lining and curtain onto the track. One-and-a-half times the track length of fabric will be needed for this tape.

Whichever tape is used, the manufacturers' instructions should be followed for the placing and stitching into position.

It is important, especially with space-pleated tapes such as triple and cartridge tapes, that the decorative pattern meets correctly in the centre and the tape is positioned accordingly.

Hand-stitched headings are obviously more time-consuming but do have advantages: they can cope with very thick and heavy interlined curtains, they can gather up more fabric to give a very luxurious effect, and they can be stitched invisibly (machine-stitched headings tend to show, particularly on plain or glossy fabrics).

Effects with tapes and tracks

Tracks and poles and heading tapes all help to determine the effect your curtains will have on the room's décor.

Heading tape is a strip of durable fabric in varying widths with integral drawstrings which are pulled up to produce a pleated effect at the curtain top. Pockets along the tape length are designed to hold the curtain hooks, ready for hanging.

There is a wide variety of tapes to choose from, including standard gathering tape, even-pleat tape, smocked and decorative tapes. The majority of these tapes can be used with any weight of curtain fabric.

They come complete with manufacturers' instructions for stitching to the curtain top. Be sure to place the tape so that the hook pockets are in the correct position for hanging from your chosen track or pole. Pull up the drawstrings evenly, thread with hooks between 8 cm to 10 cm apart and hang. Do not cut off the excess drawstrings, but knot them together in a bundle at the top of the curtain. Before laundering the curtains, remove the hooks and pull out the drawstrings so the curtains can be washed flat.

Tracks and poles can be plain or decorative – whichever is most compatible with your décor; they can also be painted or covered with matching wallpaper. Once the colour or design has been chosen, it is just a matter of making sure that the track is compatible with the weight of the fabric.

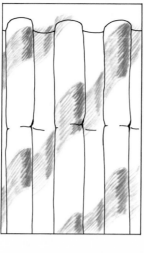
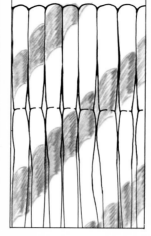
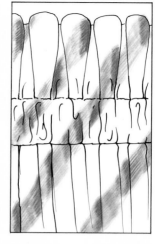
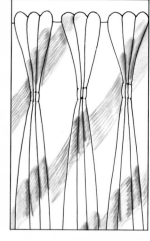

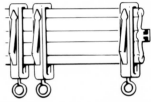
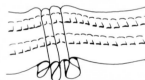

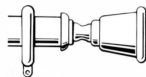

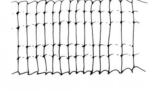

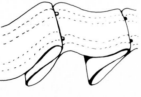

Cartridge pleat tape
This type of heading tape pulls up the curtains into evenly-spaced rounded cartridge pleats. Although it can be used with most fabrics, it is particularly good with heavy-weight fabrics such as velvets and brocades. As the pleats are spaced, it is important to position the tape so the pleats will match across the top of two curtains when they meet. Twice to 2½ times the track length of fabric is needed for this tape.

Pencil pleat tape
This type is perhaps the most popular of the heading tapes. It pulls the fabric up to form even pencil pleats. This tape can be used on all fabric weights and comes in a variety of widths, including an underslung tape for use with a curtain pole. Also available is a spaced pencil pleat tape. Between 2¼ and 2½ times the track length of fabric is needed for this tape.

Standard tape
The simplest and cheapest form of heading tape, this type merely gathers the fabric. Use it under pelmets or in kitchens and bathrooms. It looks best with lightweight, unlined curtains and just 1½ times the track length of fabric is needed.

Triple pleat tape
When stitching this tape, work from where the curtains will meet outwards so that the groups of pleats are evenly spaced and the curtain tops match across each curtain. Twice the track length of fabric is needed for this tape.

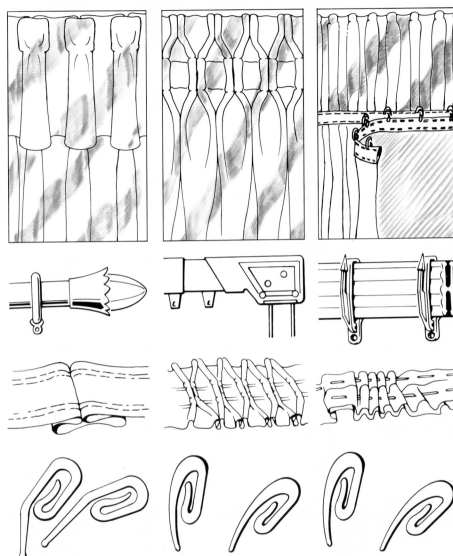

Box pleat tape
When this heading tape is pulled up the curtain top folds into evenly-spaced box pleats. Because of the pleat width this works well with heavier, lined curtains. As with cartridge pleat tape, the pulled-up heading must match across adjoining curtains, so allow for this when calculating the amount of tape needed. You will need roughly 2½ times the track length of fabric.

Smocked tape
One of a range of decorative heading tapes, this type cleverly gives the fabric top a smocked effect. It is most suited to sheer fabrics but can be used on most other curtaining fabrics. Twice the track length of fabric is required for this tape.

Lining tape
Specially made for detachable linings, this tape splits in two halves to hold the lining fabric firmly in place. The hooks feed through the lining tape into the curtain tape and then onto the track.

▲ This photograph shows a full-length curtain with pencil pleat heading tape hanging, to great effect, from a simple silver curtain track.

If you don't want to buy one of the many commercial heading tapes available, you can hand-stitch your own pleats across the curtain tops. The hooks necessary can be purchased singly in a variety of styles and stitched to the back of the pleat.

▲ A pencil-pleated top adds to the crispness of striped cotton curtains. Here the pole is mounted high above the french windows, allowing the curtains to be brought over the open door.

Measuring for curtains

- First fix your curtain track above the window, as it is the curtain track you measure, not the window.
- Decide on the heading tape you want to use (see page 62) so that you can work out how many track lengths of fabric you need for this type of tape.
- Divide this measurement by the fabric width to find how many widths of fabric will cover the track with the chosen heading.
- To find the length of each fabric drop, measure from the track to the sill, adding 5 cm to 10 cm or, if the sill protrudes, deduct 1.5 cm. For long curtains, measure from the track to the floor and deduct 1.5 cm to allow the curtain to clear the floor. To this measurement add the allowances for base hems and top (taking into

1. Measure from the track to the sill or floor, then add or deduct allowances.

account the heading tape you are using) to find the length of the drop.

If the fabric is patterned you will also need to add the length of one pattern repeat for each drop, after the first one.

● Multiply the length of the drop by the number of fabric widths to find the amount of fabric you need.

● The amount of heading tape will be the width of the curtain plus extra for turnings and for positioning the tape correctly. This is particularly important for cartridge and triple-pleat headings so that the curtain heading tapes will match across the curtains.

Preparing and cutting fabric

This is one of the most important aspects of curtain making and should not be ignored. Curtains will only hang well if the grain is straight across the fabric. And, make sure the pattern matches.

● Before you cut the first curtain length you must straighten the edge of the fabric along the grain. With woven cottons or cotton mixtures, simply snip into the selvedge at right angles to the edge and tear across the fabric from the snip to the opposite selvedge. With woven wools and linens, snip into the fabric and find a loose weft thread. Ease this out of the fabric with a pin then cut along the line made by the gap in the fabric.

● After cutting a straight edge, check

▲ Here are three examples of different cutting methods. With a matted fabric like felt (centre) it does not matter which way you cut it; it has no right or wrong side. But there are two schools of thought as to which way velvet (left) should be cut: with the pile running up or down. Normally, you cut with the pile running down, but if plain velvet is being used you will

lose the fabric's characteristic rich sheen. The crucial point is to be consistent, and when cutting several widths of velvet it is advisable to mark the top of each length as you go so that you can see at a glance which way the pile runs. Gabardine (right) is relatively easy to cut. To straighten the raw edge, follow the pattern weave to cut across the fabric width.

that the grain is straight and, if necessary, pull the fabric across the bias until it lies smooth and flat when folded in half lengthways with the selvedges together. Finally, press the entire fabric length.

● On plain fabrics, simply measure the first length up from the straight cut edge and mark across the fabric using a metre stick and either tailors' chalk or pins. Cut across along the marked line. Repeat for each length.

● Cut out any half-widths of fabric by folding the fabric in half lengthways, with selvedges together. Holding the fabric flat, slip the cutting scissors inside and carefully cut up along the fabric fold.

● On patterned fabrics, mark and cut along the straight of grain first. However, if the patterned motif is large and has been badly printed on the fabric, cut according to the motifs. In curtain making, always place the motifs along the base edge of the curtain, as any half motifs will be obscured at the top edge by the gathering produced by the heading

tape. Mark the base of the pattern repeat, then measure the allowance for the hem below the mark. Cut along this line. This will ensure that the motif will be positioned at the base edge of the curtain.

● After cutting the first length, place the cut length against the uncut fabric, matching up the pattern across both widths. Mark and cut off the second length to match. Repeat for each fabric length. Cut out any half-widths as for plain fabrics.

● After cutting out each length, mark the top edge. This is important on nap fabrics such as velvet or on some abstract-patterned fabrics.

When making velvet curtains, the direction of the fabric pile is a personal decision. On plain velvets if the pile runs down the curtains, you will lose the richness of the colour. If this is important to the room's décor, cut the curtains with the pile running upwards. In either case, remember to mark the top edge of each length as you cut it out, so they will be stitched together in the correct direction.

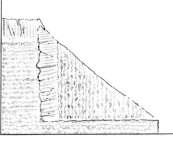

Bias Fold selvedge at right angles across fabric parallel to weft.

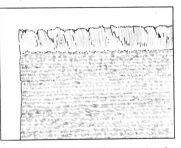

Selvedge Non-fraying tightly woven edge of fabric, parallel with warp.

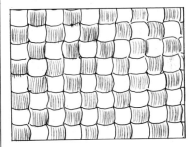

Warp Parallel strands of fibres running the length of the fabric.

Weft Strands of fibres running from side to side across fabric width.

▲ Tiered café curtains create a charming window treatment in a bedroom — use a simple heading tape for the unlined curtains and hang from fine poles.

▶ Banish the traditional nets and replace them with flowery-patterned sheer curtains. Here soft unstructured pleats are achieved with a standard heading tape hidden under a plain pelmet. Continue the light and airy feel by giving the curtains extra length.

Unlined curtains

Perfect for kitchens or bathrooms or when using sheer fabrics, unlined curtains are quick and easy to make. And, by picking the right heading tape, they can be smart too.
• Prepare and cut out all the fabric lengths as described above, allowing 15 cm for the base hem and top heading and 4 cm for each of the side hems.
• Either cut the selvedge from both sides of each fabric length and discard or simply snip into the selvedge at about 10 cm intervals along the complete length. If the tightly woven selvedge is not removed or released, it will pull the curtains into puckers along the seamlines.
• To join plain fabric lengths, place each length with right sides together; pin, tack and stitch with flat fell seams, remembering to take 1.5 cm seam allowance.
If there are any half-widths to be joined, position these on the outside edge of the curtains. To join patterned fabric lengths together, it is advisable to tack them together with ladder stitch from the right side of the fabric to gain a perfect pattern match across the seamline, before stitching together in the usual way with flat fell seams.
• After stitching all widths together, press the seams well. Turn in the side edges for 2 cm and press. Turn up the hem edge for 5 cm and press.
• To mitre the corners where the two hems are of unequal width, measure twice the hem width above folded hem edge and mark with a pin. Measure in twice the side hem width from folded side edge and mark with a pin. Fold in the corner point from pin to pin over the single hems and press well.
• Turn in a further 2 cm down side edges and press. Turn up a further 5 cm along hem edge and press. You will find that the folded edges will meet neatly at the corner. Pin and slipstitch the folded edges together across each corner.
• Using matching thread, pin, tack and slipstitch down the side hems and along the base hem, with small invisible stitches. Take care that the stitches do not show on the right side of the fabric.
• Place the curtain flat with right side facing. Measure up from the base hem edge the correct length of the curtain and mark across the curtain width using metre stick and tailors' chalk or pins. Press the excess fabric to the wrong side along this marked line.
• Trim off excess fabric to within 1 cm of folded edge (this measurement depends on the heading tape) and pin in place.
• Place heading tape against top folded edge following the manufacturers' instructions for correct position and leaving sufficient to turn under each side to neaten. Pin in place.
• Check that when pulled the gathered headings will match together across the top of the curtains.
• At the inside edge of the curtain, pull out the heading tape cords on the underside of the tape and knot each one (fig 1).
• Fold this raw edge of tape under for 1 cm, including the knotted cords, trimming if necessary.
• On the outside edge, turn under the raw edge of the heading tape, pulling the cords out from the front of the curtain tape. Leave the cords hanging freely.
• Tack and stitch heading tape in place, keeping cords free on the outside edge of the curtain, and following the stitching lines if they are marked on the tape.
To prevent the tape from puckering, always stitch on the heading tape along both the top and the bottom edges, working in the same direction.
• Pull up heading tape cords together (fig 2) until the curtain is the correct width for your track and the top has formed into neat, even pleats.
• Knot the pulled up cords together (fig 3), but do not cut off, as when the curtains need cleaning you will have to release the top heading to flatten the curtain.
• Either wind the cords together into a neat bundle or wind round a cord tidy which will slot into the heading tape.
• Thread curtain hooks through the heading tape at about 8 cm intervals with a hook positioned at each end of the curtain.
• Fit as many gliders onto the track as you have hooks on the curtains, then simply slide the hooks through the gliders. Or hang curtain directly on track with combined hook/gliders (fig 4).
• Finally, pull the curtains across the window to check that they fit without straining. Loosen or tighten the heading tape cords to fit.

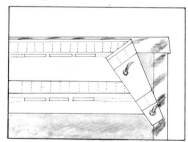
1 Knot the heading tape cords on the underside of the tape, then turn under.

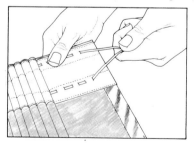
2 To form even pleats, pull up heading tape cords equally.

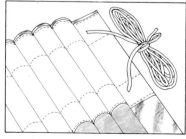
3 Wind the excess cords into a neat bundle and hold with an elastic band.

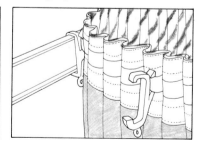
4 Some modern tracks combine hooks and gliders for easy hanging.

▲ A section of a room may be screened off with a wall of brilliant fabric. Here the curtain top is gathered into pencil-pleats, hung from a curtain pole and drawn back with self-fabric ties.

Detachable linings

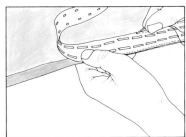

These linings can be made up after the curtains and simply added during the winter months for extra insulation.

● Prepare, cut out and make up the curtain lining in the same way as for unlined curtains, except top edge.

● Measure the length of the lining so that it will be 2.5 cm shorter than the curtain fabric. Mark across width.

● If using a pocketed tape (fig 1), cut across the curtain at marked line and slip the lining top in between the two parts of the tape. Pin, tack and stitch in place.

● If using a flat lining tape (fig 2), cut across the lining 1 cm above the marked line. Fold the excess fabric to the wrong side along marked line and position tape to top folded edge over turned-down hem. Pin, tack and stitch in place.

● In both cases, if the curtains are long, it may be necessary to catch the lining to the curtain at about 30 cm intervals down the side edges and down the seams. Either use lengths of narrow cotton tape stitched on the inside edge of the side hems and tied into loose bows, or use lengths of tape with poppers or touch and close spots sewn on the ends.

● Slide the hooks through the lining tape before the curtain heading tape so the two layers are held together with just one set of hooks (fig 3).

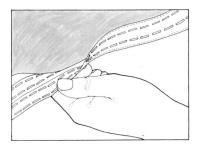

1 Lining tape opens so the fabric can be enclosed between the two halves.

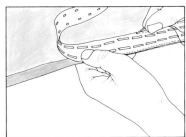

2 Stitch flat lining tape to top folded edge over turned-down hem.

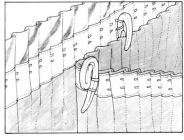

3 Slide the curtain hooks through lining tape then through heading tape.

4 With combined hooks and gliders use standard hooks and fit into eyelets.

'Locked-in' lined curtains

The professional way to make lined curtains is to lockstitch the fabric to the lining with wrong sides together.

- Prepare and cut out the fabric as for unlined curtains, but allowing a 15 cm base hem and 6.5 cm side hems.
- Prepare and cut out the lining in the same way, but 15 cm shorter and 13 cm narrower than the size of the fabric size.
- Pin, tack and stitch the fabric widths together with plain flat seams, taking 1.5 cm seam allowance. Press 6.5 cm in down both side edges. Turn and press up hem edge for 15 cm.
- Unfold and mitre each base corner (fig 1): measure in twice the side hem width from the edge and pin. Measure twice hem width above the hem edge and pin. Fold in corner from pin to pin, refold hems in place.
- Curtain weights can be added at this stage (fig 2). Circular weights are stitched to the curtain fabric inside the mitred corner, as if sewing on a button, using matching thread. Weights should also be stitched at the base of each seam. Alternatively, a length of fabric-encased weights may be used (fig 3).
- Cut a length as long as the hem and stitch the fabric together at each end to enclose the weights. Lay the weights inside the hem, catching them in place along the hem at evenly-spaced intervals.

In each case, after placing the weights, fold the hems back in place. After adding weights, slipstitch the mitred corner edges together.

- Pin, tack and herringbone stitch down the side and along the base hems, making sure the stitches do not show on right side of fabric.
- Place the curtain with wrong side up and mark the centre all down the curtain length. Mark lines 30 cm apart on either side of the centre line.
- With wrong sides facing, centre the lining over the curtain with raw edges of lining matching top, side and hem edges of fabric curtain. Pin lining and fabric together down centre mark.
- Using thread that matches the fabric, fold back the lining against the pins and lockstitch to the fabric down the centre line, beginning 10 cm from top raw edges and working down the curtain to within 2 cm of top of fabric hem (fig 4).
- Pin lining and fabric together at the next marked line on one side of the centre line and repeat the lockstitching. Continue in this way working out from the centre both ways across the fabric until the two fabrics have been lockstitched together at each marked line.
- Pin and tack fabric and lining together along the top edge. If necessary, trim lining at sides till level with curtain edge.
- Turn in side edges of lining for 2 cm. Trim if necessary, then turn up hem edge for 5 cm; press and pin.
- Slipstitch lining hems to curtain along side and hem edges with small invisible stitches (fig 5). Turn down top edges of lining and fabric together and stitch heading tape in place as for unlined curtains.

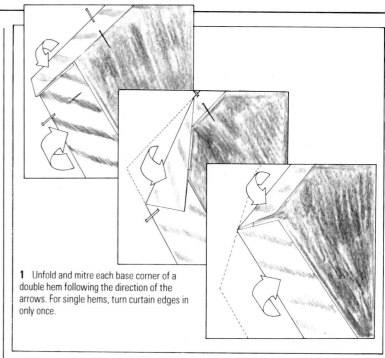

1 Unfold and mitre each base corner of a double hem following the direction of the arrows. For single hems, turn curtain edges in only once.

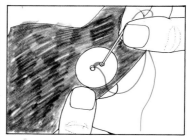

2 Available in three sizes, these weights are stitched like buttons.

3 Fabric-enclosed weights are also sold with three different-sized weights.

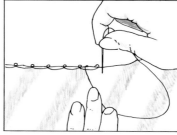

4 Lockstitch lining to fabric using thread that matches the fabric.

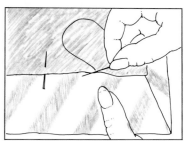

5 Slipstitch lining hems to fabric hems with invisible stitches.

▶ A simple smocking heading tape completes this long-line valance which is held over the curtain pole with lengths of curtain braid. Lining and interlining give the curtains body and they have been topped with a plain heading tape, hidden under the valance.

Interlined curtains

For a luxurious finish, add a layer of interlining between the curtain and the lining. Interlining will give added insulation and prolong the life of the curtain.

● Prepare, cut out and stitch fabric widths together as for lined curtains. Prepare, cut out and join widths of lining together in the same way as for locked-in linings. Prepare and cut out widths of interlining in the same way as for the lining fabric.

● To join widths of interlining together to gain the width of the curtain, overlap the long edges for 1 cm and herringbone stitch together.

● Lay the curtain wrong side up and mark lines for lockstitching 30 cm to 40 cm apart across the fabric in the same way as for locked-in lined curtains. Place interlining on top of curtain, matching outer raw edges.

● Pin together down the marked centre of the curtain. Fold back one half of the interlining and lockstitch to the curtain. Repeat lockstitching both ways across the curtain.

● Tack interlining and fabric together round the outer edge.

● Turn in side edges for 5 cm and turn up hem edge for 12 cm. Mitre the corners as for locked-in lined curtains. If the fabric is very thick, trim away the interlining from behind the mitred corner. Slipstitch mitred edges of corner together.

● Add curtain weights, if desired, at this stage, inside the hem.

● Herringbone stitch down side and along bottom hem edges, making sure that a fabric thread is picked up with every stitch and the hems are not just stitched to the interlining.

● Place lining with wrong side down over interlined side of curtain, matching raw edges of lining to hemmed edges of curtain, and top raw edges together.

● Pin together 2 cm away from the centre lockstitching. Fold back lining and lockstitch to the interlining along this mark and again at 30 cm to 40 cm intervals across the curtain, avoiding the previous rows of lockstitching. Work from 10 cm down from top raw edges to just above top of hem edge of curtain.

● Turn in side edges of lining for 2 cm, then turn up hem edge for 5 cm

and press. Pin and tack hems in place.

● Slipstitch lining hems to curtain hems.

● At the top edge, after marking the curtain length and trimming away the excess fabric, trim off the interlining level with the fold edge of the fabric and lining.

● Turn down fabric and lining and add heading tape as before.

'Bagged-out' lined curtains

An alternative method is to cut and make up curtain and lining widths as for unlined curtains, but with the lining 8 cm shorter and 4 cm narrower than the curtain.

● Mark the centre of fabric then lining at top and bottom of curtain.

● Place the curtain and lining with right sides together, top edges level and side edges matching.

● Pin, tack and stitch side edges together with plain, flat seams, taking 1.5 cm seam allowance to within 20 cm 'of base edge.

● After stitching, snip into seam allowance at 10 cm intervals down the complete length of the seam.

● Turn up a double 2.5cm hem along the base edge of lining. Pin, tack and stitch.

● Turn up a double 5cm hem along the base edge of curtain, mitring the corners.

● Slipstitch along hem edge. Turn curtain to the right side. Press curtain, matching centres, so there will be a

2 cm margin of fabric on wrong side of the curtain down both side edges.
• Complete the side edges of the lining by slipstitching the folded edges of the unstitched section to the curtain.
• Tack curtain and lining together along top edge and apply a heading tape as for locked-in lined curtains.

Cased headings

This is the ideal method for hanging sheer curtains, either on a length of covered wire, with screw eyes added

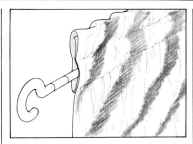

1. Push covered wire through the casing and screw a hook into the wire at each end.

to each end and fastened into screw hooks fixed into the window surround, or by threading the curtain onto rods or poles or onto fine plastic tracking. The fabric can be held completely flat against the glass or have up to one and a half times the width for fullness.
• Prepare and cut out the fabric widths as before.

• If fabric widths need to be stitched together to gain the curtain width, join with flat fell seams.
• If the side edges need neatening, turn a double 6 mm hem down each side edge; pin, tack and stitch in place.

Always use double hems on sheer fabrics as this is the best way of disguising the raw edges of the fabric.
• At the top edge, turn over a double 2 cm hem; pin, tack and stitch in place to form a casing/hem.
• Repeat, to stitch a casing along the base edge in the same way.

If hanging from a rod or pole, measure the diameter of the rod or pole first and make a casing large enough to fit round it.
• Thread the covered wire through the casings; cut to size and add a hook to each end.

Scallop headings

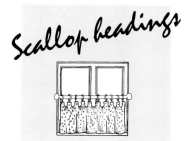

These are a more decorative form of heading, mostly used for café curtains, where large curtain rings secure the curtain onto a holding rod across the window.
• For the scallop, prepare the fabric, cut out and make up the curtains as for unlined curtains, leaving an extra 1.5 cm at the top edge.
• Divide up the width of the top edge to see how many scallops can be fitted into it. As a general guide, an 8 cm-wide scallop with a 2 cm-wide band in between is a good size.
• Mark out the positions of the scallops and then divide the remaining fabric into two equal parts for the end bands.
• Make a paper pattern of the scallop edge or at least a section of two or three scallops together, and use this to mark round on the fabric.
   The scallop shape is based on a circle, so draw round a plate to gain the rounded shape or use a compass and set square (*fig 1*)
• Mark the scallops along the top edge of the curtain, 1.5 cm down from the raw edge.
• Make up a facing the same width as the curtain and 6.5 cm longer than the scallop base.
• Turn under 1.5 cm along the base edge of the facing and press.
• Place the facing against the curtain top with right sides together. Pin, tack and stitch together all round the

shaped edge. Trim the seam allowance. snipping round the curves where necessary (*fig 2*).

• Turn the facing to the wrong side. pressing the seam to the edge. Stitch across the facing along the folded edge.

• Blanket stitch curtain rings to the centre of each band (*fig 3*) and to the end bands and then simply thread onto the curtain pole.

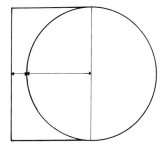

1 Mark out a pattern for the scallop shape and use it for cutting out.

2 Stitch the facing to the curtain top round the scallop-shaped edge.

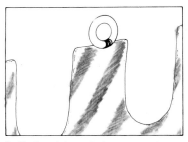

3 Blanket stitch curtain ring to centre of each band, ready for hanging.

◄ The curtain pole is mounted inside the window recess to hang the scalloped curtain flat against the window. The curtain pole should match the colour of the window frame.

▲ A simple cased-headed curtain across the centre of a bathroom window will provide privacy. This leaves the attractively-shaped window free from incumbent curtains.

Loop headings

Loop headings have fabric loops that are threaded onto a holding rod. For a straight loop top. divide the edge of the fabric up to find a good size for the loops. When you have decided on your loop size. making sure that it will go round the holding rod. for each loop cut out two pieces to the required size. plus seam allowance all round.

• Place the loops together in pairs with right sides together. Pin. tack and stitch side seams. Trim and turn through to the right side.

• Prepare the fabric. cut out and make up the curtain as for unlined curtains. but make the top edge straight and 1.5 cm longer.

• Fold the loops in half and place at each end of the curtain 1.5 cm from the outer edges.

• Place the remaining loops equally spaced (at about 8 cm intervals) between the two outer tabs.

• Cut out and make up straight facing 6 cm deep and the same width as the curtain. Turn 1.5 cm to the wrong side along base edge of facing and press.

• Place facing against curtain top with right sides together. Pin. tack and stitch side and along top edges. catching in ends of loops.

• Trim and turn the facing to the wrong side. Stitch across base edge of facing to hold it in position.

• Thread loops onto holding rod.

Trimmings

Swags and tails, valances, pelmets and tie-backs are decorative window dressings that can make all the difference to a room's décor. Tie-backs, for instance, add visual interest to a window, as well as performing the practical function of holding back the curtains and letting as much light as possible into the room. They can be made easily and quickly from off-cuts of the curtain fabric or in a contrasting fabric, stiffened with a layer of interfacing – either the modern iron-on type or the more traditional sewn-in stiffening. Curtain rings, stitched to either end, hook in place to the wall or window frame, neatly catching the curtains back on either side of the window. Tie-backs can be straight or curved; lined, interfaced or all-fabric; edged in piping or lace – the style you choose should bear some relation to the décor of the room and the curtains to be held back.

Pelmets are lengths of stiffened fabric covering the tops of curtains. There are two main methods of making a pelmet: a modern way using a special self-adhesive pelmet stiffener; and a more traditional way which will give a luxurious padded finish. Either way, the pelmet is mounted onto a pelmet board – similar to a shelf – above the window. Apart from their decorative function, pelmets are useful for concealing ugly curtain tracks. Valances perform the same functions and are usually gathered. Pelmets and valances help to balance out the proportions of a room: a shallow pelmet will give the illusion of extra height in a room with a high vaulted ceiling,

while shaped-edged pelmets are most suitable for tall, narrow windows and plain designs for wide, short windows. The simplest pelmet design is a straight box shape which can be relieved by shaped ends, a curved centre, crenellations or scallops. A valance shape will be determined largely by the choice of heading tape: a long tape will automatically frill the edge, whereas a triple-pleat heading will produce a more formal effect.

Swags and tails provide another decorative window surround, either combined with curtains or used on their own. When used in conjunction with a curtain pole, the fabric can be looped over the pole several times and held in place with touch and close fastenings – a bonus for the non-sewer.

Modern pelmets

These are made with the aid of pelmet stiffener.

As a general rule, allow for 4 cm of pelmet depth for each 30 cm length of curtain (fig 1).

Pelmets are usually mounted on a pelmet board. This looks like a wooden shelf and consists of 15 mm to 25 mm-thick plywood cut 100 mm wide and 50 mm longer than the curtain track. This shelf is fixed in place between 5 cm to 8 cm above the window on small brackets (fig 2). To give the return (the side section of the pelmet) smooth corners, cut two 100 mm squares of plywood and pin to each end of the shelf.

- The pelmet can be fixed to the edge of the pelmet board in a variety of ways (fig 3):

a Stick curtain rings to end of pelmet and hook to board over two nails.

b Fasten pelmet to board with drawing pins or tacks and cover heads with a decorative braid.

c Stick pelmet to board with a strip of Velcro at each end.

d Stitch a length of tape to the back of the pelmet forming pockets and push drawing pins through the pockets into the board at 10 cm intervals.

- To make a pattern, first fix the pelmet board in place above the window. Use a length of brown paper the same length as the edge of the pelmet board and the desired depth (work this out proportionally as it can always be altered at this stage if it does not look quite right).

- Fold the paper in half widthways and then mark and cut out your design. Unfold the pattern.

- Temporarily fix to the board with pins to check and alter if necessary. Then remove and add the return (side) sections to either end.

- Cut out the fabric widths and join together if necessary with flat seams.

- Position the seams on either side of a central fabric width and match up any pattern by ladderstitching the fabrics together before stitching the seams. Make up the lining to fit in the same way.

- Place pattern on fabric and cut out adding 1.5 cm seam allowance all round the pelmet shape. Repeat, to cut out the lining.

- Using the pattern, cut out a strip of pelmet stiffener, omitting to add the seam allowance.

- Lay the fabric wrong side up. Peel the backing from one side of the stiffener and, placing centrally against wrong side of fabric, smooth in place.

- Peel backing from the top side of stiffener. Turn back seam allowance of fabric and stick to stiffener, clipping into curves if necessary (fig 4).

- Turn in seam allowance all round pelmet lining, snipping into allowance on corners and curves.

- Place lining over pelmet with wrong sides together, matching outer edges.

- Slipstitch folded edges together, making sure lining does not show on right side of pelmet (fig 5).

- Decide on a method of fastening and attach to back of pelmet and to pelmet board. Fix pelmet in place.

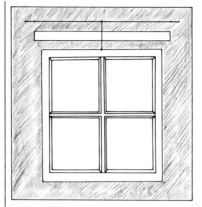

1 Measure length and depth of curtain track, adding 5cm. Fix the board 5-8cm above window frame.

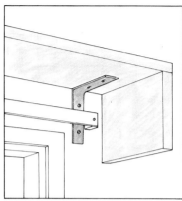

2 Fix pelmet shelf above window on small brackets. To gain sharp corners, add sides.

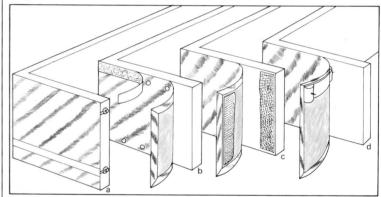

3a Stitch curtain rings to end of pelmet and hook to board over two nails. **3b** Fasten pelmet to board with drawing pins or tacks and cover the heads with a decorative braid. **3c** Stick pelmet to board with a strip of Velcro at each end. **3d** Stitch a length of tape to the back of the pelmet forming pockets and push drawing pins through the pockets into the board at 10cm intervals.

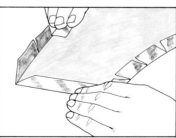

4 Turn seam allowance of fabric to wrong side of stiffener and press in place.

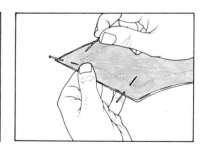

5 Slipstitch lining all round pelmet, taking small invisible stitches.

▲ Unusually-shaped pelmets are easy to make with modern materials. First draw up a pattern and then make sure it will fit.

Traditional pelmets

Make up your pattern in the same way as for modern pelmets. Then, using your pattern, cut out sufficient lengths of fabric, interlining and lining in the same way as for modern pelmets, adding 1.5 cm seam allowance all round.

• Place interlining to wrong side of fabric and lockstitch together at 30 cm to 40 cm intervals across the pelmet in the same way as for interlined curtains.

• Using the pattern, cut out buckram stiffener without adding seam allowance. Place buckram centrally against wrong side of interlined pelmet. Pin and tack together.

• Fold fabric seam allowance over buckram and herringbone stitch fabric to buckram all round the pelmet, clipping into curves if necessary.

• Turn in seam allowance all round lining; pin and tack. Place lining with wrong side to buckram side of fabric, matching folded edges. Pin and slipstitch folded edges together.

• Fix to pelmet board, using one of the methods outlined.

Valances

Valances are made up with a heading tape in the same way as curtains.

Special valance rails can be hooked onto the curtain track and the valance can then be hung from this rail over the curtain. Alternatively, it can be fixed to the front of a pelmet board in a variety of ways (*fig 1*): by fixing screw eyes into the front edge of the board and hooking the valance on with conventional curtain hooks, or by pinning it to the front edge of the board, hiding the drawing pins among the gathered folds.

• Either add a valance rail to your existing track or fix up a pelmet shelf.

• Prepare and cut out the required number of fabric widths. Ladder-stitch together from the right side to match the pattern, then stitch together taking 1.5 cm seam allowance with plain flat seams. Press seams open.

• Repeat to make up the lining in the same way, but cut it 5cm smaller all round than the fabric.

• On the fabric, turn in side edges for 4 cm and press. Turn up hem edge for 4 cm and press. Mark the corner point with a pin. Unfold hem and side edges. Press in the corner at right angles through corner point, where pin is positioned.

• Refold the corner with right sides together. Pin, tack and stitch across pressed line to within 1.5 cm of raw edges. Trim and carefully turn out the corner to the right side. Repeat with second corner.

• Place the lining with right sides together, matching seams. Pin, tack and stitch along base edge, taking 1.5 cm seam allowance, continuing stitching up both side edges. Trim and turn the valance to the right side.

• Press down raw edges of the fabric and lining together.

• Stitch a heading tape to the top folded edges as for curtains and pull up evenly to fit.

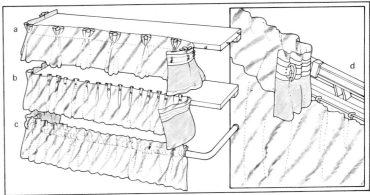

1a Hang with curtain hooks through screw eyes fixed into the edge. **1b** Fasten valance in position with drawing pin fixed in place through back of pleats. **1c** Stitch a top casing and thread into a rail. **1d** Hang the valance on a valance rail fixed to the front of the curtain track.

▲ The perfect complement to a curtain — the border section of the fabric is used here for the tie-back, the top and bottom edged with two rows of covered piping, one to match the fabric and one in a contrasting colour, matching up with the curtain edge.

Lined tie-backs

Lined tie-backs, suitable for heavy fabrics, give a more professional finish because of the invisible hand stitching.

• To find the finished length of a tie-back, hold a tape measure round the curtain at the desired height, creating the folded effect you want, then hold back against the wall (*fig 1*). As well as gauging the length of the tie-back, mark on the wall the position of the holding hook.

• To decide on the width, cut out a rough paper shape and pin it round the curtain to see the effect, altering the width until it looks in the right proportion for the curtain.

• In all cases, apart from plain, stiffened interfacing in the centre, or your chosen tie-back. Fold and cut the pattern in half widthways, then cut out placed to the fabric fold. Cutting out in this way ensures that two shaped tie-backs will be equal.

• To make up tie-backs, either cut both sides from the fabric adding a stiffened interlining in the centre, or cut one shape from the fabric, one from the lining and one from the stiffening.

Measure and make up a pattern for the tie-back.

• Using the pattern, cut one piece from the fabric and one piece from the lining. Cut out one piece of heavyweight interfacing, 1.5 cm smaller all round than the fabric and lining. Pin the interfacing centrally to wrong side of fabric tie-back.

• Fold the fabric edges over the interfacing. Pin, tack and herringbone stitch the turned-back edges to the interfacing (*fig 2*).

• Fold in 1.5 cm seam allowance to the wrong side all round the lining tie-back, press and tack in place, clipping into sharp corners and curves as necessary.

• Place wrong side of lining against interfaced side of fabric tie-back, matching outer fold edges.

• Slipstitch folded edges together all round the tie-back, being careful not to let the lining show on the right side of the tie-back (*fig 3*).

• Position a curtain ring at each end of the tie-back against the lining, so that the ring just overlaps the side edge. Blanket stitch the ring into position (*fig 4*).

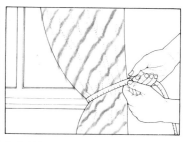

1 Hold the tape measure round curtain to gauge length and position of tie-back.

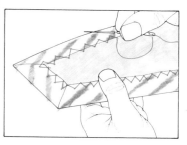

2 Herringbone stitch fabric to stiffening to gain a sharp outer edge.

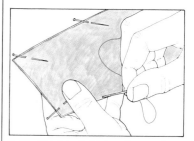

3 Slipstitch lining to fabric making sure the lining does not show on right side.

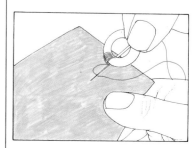

4 Just overlap the edge with the curtain ring and blanket stitch in place.

All-fabric tie-backs

All-fabric tie-backs are machine-stitched and more suitable for lighter-weight fabrics.

- Measure and make up a pattern for the tie-back. Using the pattern, cut out two pieces from the fabric. Cut out one piece from iron-on heavyweight interfacing, 1.5 cm smaller than the pattern all round.
- Place the interfacing centrally, adhesive side down on the wrong side of one fabric piece. Iron into position.
- Place second fabric piece against first, right sides together. Pin, tack and stitch together all round the edge of the interfacing, leaving an opening in one side edge (*fig 1*). Trim and turn tie-back to the right side.
- Turn in opening edges in line with the rest of the seam. Slipstitch together to close.
- Fix a curtain ring to each end of tie-back, in the same way as for lined tie-backs.

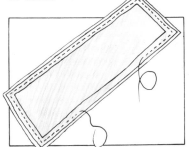

1 Stitch together all round, leaving a central opening in one long side.

▲ To add to the effect of standard-headed curtains mounted behind the curtain pole complete with decorative finals, a length of matching fabric has been looped over the curtain pole in regular-shaped loops. To provide further definition, a deep contrasting fringe has been added to the hanging edges.

▶ Here gentle loops of fabric are combined with more formal shaped tails hanging between the windows. The fabric is edged with a slightly gathered frill and a band of plain fabric that outlines and emphasizes the two distinctive shapes.

Blinds

Blinds are the cheapest and easiest way to cover a window with fabric. Of the various types of blind (roller. Roman. festoon. Austrian). the simplest type is the roller blind which is wound round a wooden roller with a spring mechanism to raise and lower the fabric. Any fabric able to wind successfully round the roller can be used for a roller blind. Sheers and lace are particularly effective when used as an alternative to net curtains. Blinds made from furnishing fabric can be stiffened with a special spray or fused with a layer of woven interfacing. A special pre-stiffened fabric intended for roller blinds can be bought in wide widths and made up quickly and easily (no side hems) into a smart window covering. The base edge of a roller blind can be finished in a variety of ways. from a plain stitched casing for the batten to scallops or a fringe. The batten provides both a firm edge and a base for

the cord and acorn used to trigger the roller mechanism.

Like roller blinds when lowered. Roman blinds lie flat against the window. but when raised. pull up into neat horizontal pleats. Made from non-stiffened fabric and lined. Roman blinds are fixed to the window on a length of wooden battening. painted to merge in with the surroundings. Fine cords. running through special ring tape stitched to the back of the blind in vertical rows. provide the leverage when combined with screw eyes fixed to the bottom edge of the battening. The screw eyes bring all the cords to one side. where a cleat holds them in position.

Festoon blinds have rows of narrow heading tape stitched vertically on the reverse side of the blind. After stitching in place. these tapes are pulled up until the blind is the correct length for the window. pro-

viding a slightly gathered look. At the top. the fabric is fixed to a length of battening and the blind is raised and lowered with cords in the same way as the Roman blind. The side and hem edges can be bound with bias or contrasting fabric or a simple frill.

Austrian blinds are gathered vertically like festoon blinds and horizontally by means of a length of heading tape stitched across the top edge. (The heading tape means that they have to hang on a conventional curtain track fixed to the front of a length of battening.) The choice of heading tape will also affect the amount of gathering and. if you want to go the whole hog. an extra frill can be stitched to the base edge. Festoon and Austrian blinds are usually unlined and made from lightweight or sheer fabrics which gather up well and filter the light attractively.

Blinds can be used either combined with curtains or on their own.

▶ This blind's simple, uncluttered lines are emphasized by the use of a plain semi-transparent fabric. The unusual shape is achieved by one central pulley cord, which pulls up the fabric into large loops.

▼ There are various types of acorns to choose from. It is best to select the one most suited to the style of the blind. The tasseled type, for example, would add that finishing touch to a festoon blind.

Roller blinds

A basic roller blind is a length of fabric that hangs flat against the window on a wooden roller. Easy to clean, they tend to suit utilitarian windows in kitchens and bathrooms. To make one, you will need: a wooden roller with a square pin at one end and a round pin attached to a pin cap for hammering in at the cut end; two brackets (one to hold the square pin that operates the spring winding mechanism, the other to hold the round pin); a wooden lath to slot through the casing at the bottom of the blind; a cord holder and cord; and an acorn or ring pull attachment for lowering and raising the blind.

On a recessed window, use a metal ruler to measure horizontally from one side of the recess to the other (*fig 1*). Deduct 1.5 cm from both sides to allow for the end mechanisms.

The brackets will be positioned at these points, 3 cm down from the top of the recess to allow for the thickness of the blind when it is rolled up.

On a window without a recess, allow 2.5 cm extra on either side and 5 cm above the window.
• Mark, then fix the brackets at the window, with the round pinhole bracket on the right-hand side and the square-hole bracket on the left-hand side so that the fabric will go up behind the roller (*fig 2*).
• Cut the roller to fit.
• Place cap over the cut end and hammer in the pin, holding the roller horizontally (*fig 3*). Do not rest the roller on the spring end as this can damage the mechanism. Place roller in brackets and check for fit.
• For the amount of fabric needed, measure from the roller to the sill using a retractable, metal rule. Add 25 cm to this measurement to allow for the hem casing and for the roller still to be covered with fabric when the blind is down. For the width, measure the wooden part of the roller and add 2 cm for side hems.

If necessary, allow for centring the design and, when using a patterned fabric on extra wide windows, allow for matching the pattern across any seams. Square off the fabric before cutting out the blind.
• At each side edge, turn in edges for 1 cm. Pin, tack and zigzag stitch the edges in place, positioning zigzag stitches centrally over raw edges. When working with a straight-stitch sewing-machine work two rows of straight stitching close together down each edge.
• At the base, turn up 5 cm hem, then turn in 1 cm to form a 4 cm-wide casing for lath. Pin, tack and stitch across casing close to fold edge and down one side of casing.
• Iron the fabric well to remove all creases, then apply spray-on stiffener. Allow to dry and repeat if necessary.
• Trim wooden lath so it is 2 cm shorter than blind width. Slide into casing (*fig 4*).
• Stitch side opening to close casing and hold lath in position.
• Make up the cord pull: thread one end of cord through acorn and knot to hold in place. Pull opposite end of cord through cord holder and position to centre back of lath to check for length.
• Knot and trim off excess cord. Screw cord holder in place (*fig 5*). Press 1.5 cm to the right side along the top edge of the blind.
• Place roller on to the right side of the fabric, with spring mechanism on the left-hand side. Place folded edge of fabric along marked line of roller. Tack in place at 2 cm intervals, placing a tack at either end of the roller through the side hems (*fig 6*).
• To ensure the mechanism is at correct tension, wind up blind by hand and slot into the brackets with fabric flat against the window (*fig 7*).
• Pull down to check that it will roll up correctly; if not, remove from brackets and rewind by hand; replace in brackets.

To increase their decorative potential, roller blinds can also have shaped or trimmed edgings.

Roller blinds made from stiffened fabric

Fix the brackets in position as for basic roller blinds.
• Measure for the fabric as before, but omitting side hem allowances and allowing 4 cm only for the base hem.
• Cut out the stiffened fabric using a ruler and set square to achieve straight base and side edges.
• At the base turn up a single 4 cm-wide hem. Stitch across hem and down one side. Insert lath and close opening as before.
• At top edge, fold and hand-press 1.5 cm to the right side. Tack onto the roller as for the previous blind.
• Fix on the cord holder and acorn as before and hang the blind in the brackets.

1 Use a metal ruler to measure horizontally across a recessed window.

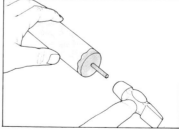

2 Position square-hole bracket on the left, and pin-hole bracket on the right.

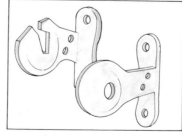

3 Cover the right-hand edge with end cap and hammer in the pin.

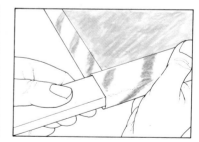

4 Slide the wooden lath into the casing and neatly stitch up open end to close.

5 Place cord holder centrally against back of lath and screw in place.

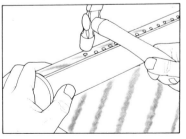

6 Fold top edge to marked line on roller, and tack in place.

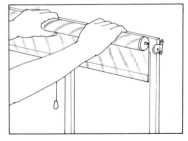

7 Hang blind with fabric flat against the window.

▲ The simple structured lines of a roller blind frame the window, while the addition of curtains will help to keep out the light. Construct both from the same fabric, matching up with the cool sophisticated colours in the room.

Roman blinds

Roman blinds are fixed to the window on a length of battening and can be made from non-stiffened fabric that is pulled up into neat, horizontal folds on cords threaded through plastic rings or thread loops on special tapes. You will need: battening, fabric, lining, plastic ring tape to sew to the back of the blind in vertical rows, staple gun and staples, nylon cord to thread through the rings, one screw eye for each row of tape; a wooden lath the width of the blind to weight the bottom edge; and a cleat to secure the cords.

In a recessed window the blind will fit into the recess against the ceiling. On a window without a recess, the battening will have to be mounted on supports that should be positioned on either side of the window at the desired height.

● Measure and cut the wooden battening to fit and fix in place. Paint the battening to match the window surround.

● For the fabric length, measure from the battening to the window sill. Add 13 cm to this measurement for base hem and for fixing to the battening.

● For the width, measure the length of the battening and add 9 cm for side hems. Cut out fabric to the correct size. Trim off selvedges.

If, to gain the blind width, it is necessary to join fabric widths

▲ Here a fine vertical lath of wood threaded through the narrow casing across the back of each blind help to emphasize the edges of the pleats when the blind is raised.

together, you can avoid having an ugly centre seam by joining two half widths of fabric to either side of a central width with plain flat seams.

• Cut out the lining to the same length as the fabric, but 9 cm narrower.

• Mark the centre of both fabric and lining at top and base edges. Place fabric to lining with right sides together. Pin, tack and stitch side seams, taking 1.5 cm seam allowance. Trim and turn to the right side.

• Match up centres at top and base edges and press down side edges, so the seamlines will lie 3 cm from the outer edge of the blind.

• At the base edge, turn up the fabric and lining together for 11 cm, turn under the raw edge for 1 cm and press. Pin the hem to hold it in position.

• Measure the width of the blind from seamline to seamline and divide equally into sections, between 25 cm and 30 cm apart. These will be the positions of the vertical tapes.

• Cut off a length of tape for each position, the length of the blind from the top to 1 cm below hem edge.

• Position the first length over one seamline, with first ring 3 cm up from hem edge. Tuck 1 cm of tape under hem edge. Stitch. Repeat to stitch second row of tape and rings over opposite seamline.

• Pin, tack and stitch remaining rows of tape in between, making sure that the sets of rings are in horizontal lines across the back of the blind (fig 1). Tuck all the raw ends inside the hem.

• Pin, tack and stitch across the top of the hem catching in the ends of tape. Stitch across hem again 4 cm from previous stitching forming a

casing for bottom lath. Zigzag stitch across raw top edges of blind, catching in raw edges of tape.

• Cut bottom lath so that it is 2 cm shorter than casing. Insert into casing. Slipstitch down sides of casing, continuing stitching across ends of hem, enclosing lath.

• Remove battening from window. Position 2 cm of the top edge of the blind over the wide side of the battening. Using a staple gun, fix the blind to the wood, positioning staples about 2 cm apart, with one at each end (fig 2).

Flat borders in a contrasting fabric can be added to the sides of the blind for a greater decorative effect, if desired.

• Fix a screw eye to the underside of the battening at the top of each vertical row of tape (fig 3).

• Measure for the pulley cords: twice the length of the blind plus one width measurement. Knot the first length of cord to the ring at the base of the first row of tape. Pass the cord up the length of tape through each ring. Repeat to thread a length of cord through all the rings on each row of tape.

• At the top, thread each length of cord through each screw eye until all the cords hang together at one side of the blind.

• Fix the battening in place at the window (fig 4).

• Mark position and fix a cleat at the side of the window. Knot the cords together level with the window sill and cut off excess.

• Pull up the blind, smoothing in the folds one on top of the other (fig 5). Wind the cords together in a figure of eight round the cleat (fig 6). Leave the blind in this position for a few days to fix the pleats in position.

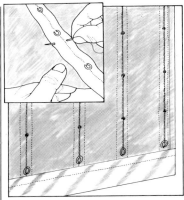

1 Stitch lengths of ringed tape vertically down the back of the blind.

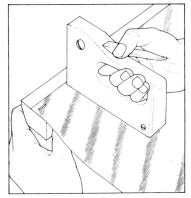

2 Staple blind to wide top edge of the battening.

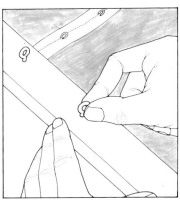

3 Fix a screw eye to underside of battening at top of each row of tape.

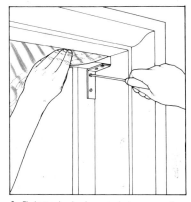

4 Fix battening in place at window on small brackets.

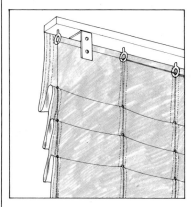

5 Pull up the blind with pulley cords to form neat, even pleats.

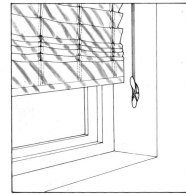

6 Wind cords round cleat in a figure of eight to hold the blind in position.

▶ A large expanse of window can be covered to great effect with a festoon blind. The clean-cut top outlines the window, while the blind base pulls up vertically into waves of fabric.

▼ Here a touch of flamboyant pattern has been added to an otherwise plain and sombre room. A neat pencil-pleat heading tape works well with the evenly-spaced horizontal gathering and the simple frill to neatly define the base edge.

Festoon blinds are fixed in place to wooden battening in the same way as Roman blinds, so cut, paint and fix supports (if necessary) for the battening in the same way.

● For the fabric, measure the length from battening to sill and add one third again for vertical gathering. For the width, measure the length of the battening, adding 4 cm for side hems.

● Cut out one fabric piece to the required size. If the window is extra wide, fabric widths will have to be joined together to gain the correct width. To do this, seam together with narrow plain flat seams, positioning so they will fall under a vertical tape.

● Round off the base corners; place a plate against the first corner matching to side and base edges. Mark round plate, remove and trim fabric along marked line. Fold fabric in half matching side edges. Mark curved corner on opposite side of blind. Unfold and trim round marked line.

● Turn a double 1 cm-wide hem down both side edges and along base edge. Pin to hold in place. Mark, measure and cut vertical tapes as for Roman blind. Position first row of tape 3 cm from outer edge. Pin, tack and stitch in place. Repeat at opposite side of blind, and at each marked position in between.

● Tuck ends of tape inside the base hem. Tack and stitch hem in place making sure that the heading tape cords are caught in place with the hem stitching. Cut a length of 4 cm-wide tape and fold in half evenly over top raw edge of blind, covering ends of tape, but leaving heading tape cords free. Pin, tack and stitch tape in place, turning under raw side edges.

● Thread curtain rings through

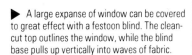

Festoon blinds are vertically gathered. They are raised and lowered by means of cords threaded through curtain rings fixed into vertical bands of narrow heading tape. When drawn up, they form ruffles at the base edge. You will need: battening, fabric, small brass rings, narrow heading tape, pulley cord, screw eyes and a cleat.

heading tape (*fig 1*), placing the first row 10 cm from bottom edge. Space the remaining rows of rings about 30 cm apart, making the last row about 15 cm from top of blind. Make sure that each set of rings makes a horizontal row across the back of the blind.

● Pull up each row of heading tape from the top of the blind to the required amount. Tie the cords into a bow at the top of each row of tape (*fig 2*).

● Cut lengths of pulley cords as for the Roman blind. Fasten the first length of cord to the bottom rings on

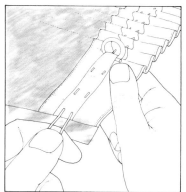

1 Thread brass curtain rings through the narrow heading tape in horizontal rows.

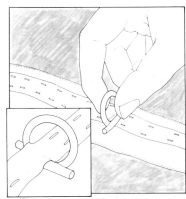

2 Pull up the vertical heading tapes from the top and tie excess cords together.

the first row of tape. Thread the cord up through all the rings above it. Repeat with each length of cord and each row of tape.

● Fix screw eyes into the underside of the battening so that they match up with each row of tape. Place taped edge of blind over the top edge of the battening and tack in place, positioning tacks about 2 cm apart and with one at each end (*fig 3*).

● Complete threading of cords and then hang blind as for Roman blind.

Austrian blinds

Austrian blinds are often confused with festoon blinds, but they differ from festoon blinds in two ways: as well as being vertically gathered, they are gathered horizontally at the top by means of heading tape and are hung from a curtain track fixed to the front edge of a length of battening.

● Measure, cut and paint battening and fix supports in place (if necessary) as for Roman blind. Fix curtain track to the narrow front edge of the battening.

● For the fabric length, measure from the curtain track/battening to the sill adding one third again for the vertical gathering. For the width, measure the width of the curtain track/battening and double it (this depends on the heading tape used).

● Cut out fabric to the required size. It may be necessary to seam fabric

widths together to gain the correct size. If this is the case, stitch together with narrow plain flat seams, positioning the seams so, they will fall under a vertical row of tape.

● Turn in both side edges to form double 1 cm hems. Pin, tack and stitch hems in place.

● To add an optional base frill, cut out sufficient fabric widths to the required depth which when stitched together will be twice the width of the base of the blind. Pin, tack and stitch frill widths together with French seams.

● Turn under base and side edges of frill to form a double 1 cm hem, carefully mitring the corners. Pin, tack and stitch in place.

● On wrong side of blind, mark positions of heading tapes with outside rows 4 cm from side edges and remaining rows about 30 cm apart in between. Cut a length of heading tape for each marked position the length of the blind, minus the frill. Pin, tack and stitch each length of tape in position.

● Work two rows of gathering stitches along top edge of frill. Place frill against base of blind with right sides together, matching side hems. Pull up gathering threads evenly to fit. Pin, tack and stitch in place taking 2 cm seam allowance on blind and 1.5 cm seam allowance on frill. Trim down frill turnings. Turn under raw edge of blind seam allowance and fold flat against the blind, catching in raw ends of tape. Pin, tack and stitch in place.

● Turn down top edge of blind for 1.5 cm. Position heading tape on wrong side of blind, 6 mm from top folded edge. At one side pull out 4 cm of heading tape cords at the back of the tape and knot. Turn

under with the raw side edge.

● At opposite side, pull out cords from the front of the tape and leave hanging free when turning under raw side edge. Making sure that the cords in the vertical tapes are free, pin, tack and stitch the heading tape in place.

● Thread curtain rings in horizontal rows across the blind, positioning first row 2 cm from frill seam and last row about 15 cm from top edge. Space the remaining rows about 30 cm apart in between. Pull up each row of tape as for festoon blind.

● Pull up top heading tape till blind is the same width as the curtain track. Knot cords at one side and wind together. Fix screw eyes into battening as for festoon blind.

● Thread curtain hooks through top heading tape with a hook at each end and the remainder spaced about 8 cm in between.

● Fix an end stop at each end of the curtain track.

● Cut pulley cords and thread up through rings as for festoon blind. Fix onto curtain track (*fig 1*). Fix up cleat and complete threading the blind as for festoon blind.

1 After threading up the blind with pulley cords, hang blind from curtain track.

Living Areas

The living room is where you get your living done, and your choice of furnishings should reflect that. This is the family forum: here the children grow up, friends are entertained; books are read and games are played. But that does not mean that it should be dour or purely functional. Matching colours and themes can mould this hub of human activity into a harmonious whole.

► Rich fabrics give a luxurious feel to a room — match up the bolsters, knotting the long ends to cushion covers. Add a heavy gold fringing to the cover base to tie the fabrics to the room's décor and colour scheme.

Room Dividers

◀ Create a grand style with a gathered ceiling, pelmets over the fireplace as well as the windows, and covered wall panels. Outline the panels with painted beading and the window pelmet with a neat braid. Using the same fabric throughout ties the whole scheme together, while the pastel paint breaks up the patterned areas and prevents it overwhelming the room.

▼ A screen need not serve a functional purpose, but can be purely decorative, perhaps (as here) to brighten a corner. Fabric paint has been used to stencil the curtain motif onto the corners of the screen to underline the screen's total integration into the scheme of the room.

Walls and ceilings are important design sections of a house and, although it is usual to cover them with paint or wallpaper, fabric may also be used – often to considerable effect. Fabric provides extra insulation for heat as well as against noise. Wide-width fabrics such as sheeting, felt and sheer fabrics can be used, but remember that when used flat the fabric will have to be exactly matched across the walls, so a large motif pattern will add considerably to the bill. Wall fabric is stapled to battening mounted to the walls, around doors and windows. And, where there is a light fitment or electric socket the fabric is treated like a wallpaper: the fittings removed and replaced over the cut fabric. Some can be pleated up beforehand, but must have sufficient body for the pleats to hold successfully. This method works best on short walls, where the pleats are less likely to fall out in the middle. The fabric can also be gathered up either with two rows of gathering threads or by means of a length of heading tape added to the top edge. A ceiling covered with fabric gives a tented effect, and again the fabric can either be kept flat or gathered up at the outer edges.

Screens have been used for many years to divide up rooms or partition off changing or washing areas. They are particularly useful in large through-rooms to separate the sitting and dining areas. If the screen is to be used to divide two rooms in this way, each side may be covered with a different fabric to match the décor of the respective rooms.

The framework of a screen will be more solid if made from a soft wood, such as pine. The fabric is simply stretched over the frame on both sides and stapled in place, while the edges are finished with a narrow beading to cover the raw fabric edges and provide a decorative edge. A screen may consist of any number of sections held together with hinges – depending on height of screen.

Screens

A screen consists of two, three or more panels, hinged together into a row. Use a soft wood such as pine for the framework, adding fabric to match the décor.

The framework of each matching panel is made from 50 mm by 25 mm planed soft wood. For each panel you will need two pieces each 600 mm long for top and base and two pieces each 1,500 mm long for frame uprights. Cut one 600 mm length to give the screen a centre support.

● With the narrow side of the wood on the outside, place one top piece against the inside edge of one upright with a right-angle join. Fix together with a plastic connecting block screwed inside the corner (fig 1).

● Lay the corner on its side and hammer a corrugated metal connector across the corner join, driving it right into the wood. Turn the section over and fix a corrugated connector across that side of the corner (fig 2). Repeat on the remaining corners to make up the complete outer frame.

● Join the centre support to both sides of the frame with the wider side of the wood facing outwards, fixing in place with plastic connecting blocks as before. Paint or varnish round the outer part of the frame section.

● Cut a piece of fabric for each side of the screen, slightly larger than the frame. With the grain running lengthways, place the fabric right side out against the frame and staple in place. Keep fabric smooth and taut as you staple. Trim off the raw edges with pinking shears just inside the edge of the frame (fig 3). Staple the fabric to the other side of the frame in the same way.

● Cut lengths of half-round beading to fit each edge of the frame, mitring the corners. Paint or varnish them if necessary.

● Stick the beading over the pinked edges of the fabric, flush with the edges of the frame (fig 4).

● Make up the remaining screen panels in the same way.

● Place two panels together and screw three hinges down the edges of the connecting sides, placing one hinge in the centre and the remaining two 10 cm from top and base edges (fig 5).

Continue in this way until all the panels are hinged together in a neat row.

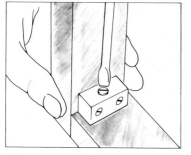

1 Screw a connecting block into each corner of the wooden frame.

2 Hammer a metal connector across each frame join from both sides.

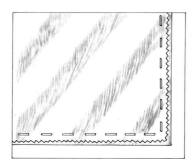

3 Staple the fabric taut to both sides of each wooden panel.

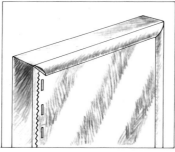

4 Cover the pinked fabric edges with lengths of half-round beading.

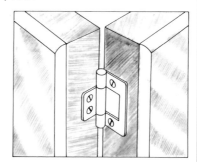

5 Hinge the completed panels together in a row.

Flat fabric walls

The easiest way to apply fabric to walls is by mounting it flat onto a special track fitted at the point where the wall meets the ceiling and along the top of the skirting board. This track consists of plastic or metal battens with a grip edge into which the material is slotted. Tracking is also fitted down the walls at each corner and around any windows, doors, electric sockets and light switches (fig 1).

● Measure and cut each length of track to fit; mark and drill holes for fixing in place. Mitre the corners where the track meets.

● Next, measure for the fabric. When covering a wide wall the fabric will have to be seamed to gain the correct width. Pin, tack and stitch together with plain flat seams.

When using patterned fabric, ladderstitch the widths together before stitching, so the pattern will match exactly.

● Peel off the protective tape from the track and, working from the centre, smooth the fabric, right side out over the top track, leaving 2.5 cm free above the track.

● Smooth the bottom edge of the fabric in place, in the same way, working into each corner. Make sure that the pattern is parallel with the skirting boards and ceiling.

Trim the fabric vertically at each corner if necessary.

● Working with a special tool supplied with the track, press overlapping fabric into the storage channel, beginning in the centre and working out towards each side (*fig 2*).

● Repeat along base edges and then down each vertical length of track in the corners or round the windows and doors.

A cheaper way of applying fabric to walls is to make your own frame using 2.5cm-wide battens cut to size and screwed to the walls. The fabric is then tacked to the battens with upholstery tacks.

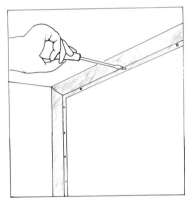

1 Fix tracking all round outer edges of walls, doors and windows.

2 Push fabric into channels of the track keeping it stretched taut.

▲ For an alternative screen, fix the wooden frame together but make up an unlined curtain for each panel. Finish the top and base edges with a casing and thread on covered wires strung between the panel sides.

▲ Create atmosphere with swathes of fabric. Fix the fabric to the walls on battens, gathering up the excess at intervals in heavy loops. Add rosettes of matching fabric at the top of each set of pleats.

Pleated fabric walls

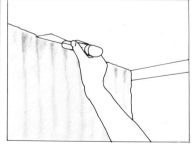

The best fabric for pleating on walls is a furnishing cotton that will crease well into sharp pleats. The fabric should be fixed in place onto 25 mm by 25 mm battening mounted on the walls.

● Fix up the battening in the same way as the track for flat fabric walls (it is not essential to mitre the corners). Leave a small 2 mm gap at the top and base edges between battening and ceiling and between battening and skirting (*fig 1*).

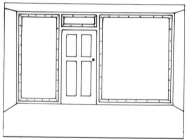

1 Leave a gap between battening and ceiling or skirting for fabric.

2 Push pleated fabric into gaps to hold firmly in place.

When measuring for fabric, decide on the width of the pleats you require and take into account the take-up for this size.

• Work out the fabric sections wall by wall, stitching fabric widths together to achieve the required size.

• Mark, then pleat up each section of fabric, pinning and tacking (using contrasting thread) down the complete length. Press well.

• Hold pleated fabric to battening and fix in place using either a staple gun and staples or hammer and tacks. Push excess fabric at top and bottom into the gaps between the battening and ceiling or battening and skirting (*fig 2*).

• Leave for a few days, then remove tacking stitches, and pleats should be fixed in position.

• Cover staples or tacks with matching or contrasting tape or braid.

Gathered fabric walls

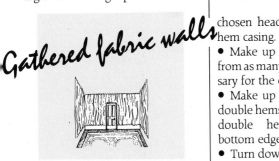

There are two ways to gather wall fabric: either stitch a heading tape to the top of the fabric so that it gathers up into even pleats, or make a casing along top edge and thread covered wire through, as for base edge.

• When using a heading tape, fix a narrow curtain track around the top of the walls only, so that when hung, the gathered curtain top will be flush with the ceiling (*fig 1*).

• Measure for fabric from the track to the top of the skirting, allowing for chosen heading tape and 6 cm for hem casing.

• Make up a curtain for each wall from as many fabric widths as necessary for the chosen heading tape.

• Make up each curtain with 1 cm double hems at each side and a 3 cm double hem/casing along the bottom edge.

• Turn down the top edge and add curtain heading tape in the same way as for unlined curtains. Pull up heading tape and hang on the track.

• Thread a length of covered wire through the hem casing and fasten to wall at each corner above skirting board with a screw eye (*fig 2*).

The curtains will meet at the corners, and any gaps will be hidden by the gathered fabric held taut.

Alternatively, make a casing at both top and base edges and thread covered wire through.

1 Fix a neat curtain track that will hold the fabric flush with the ceiling.

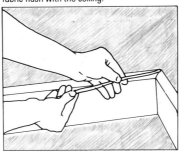

2 When gathered on a covered wire, hold in place with screw eyes.

▲ Panels of exotic fabric offer an exciting alternative to wallpaper, and will bring a plain, uninteresting room to life. Use the same fabric for lampshades and extra-large floor cushions.

Tented ceilings

Tented ceilings are most effective in a room with a central light fitting. Like wall fabric, ceiling fabric can also be held in place to battening positioned around the room.

● Mark a line at picture rail height all round the room. Position 25mm by 25mm battening around the wall along the marked line, mitring the corners. Screw in place (*fig 1*).

● To measure for the fabric in a square room, measure from the centre point of the ceiling down to one corner, then measure to the next corner, forming a large triangle (*fig 2*). Make a pattern to this size and cut out four triangles. If the triangle is too large for the fabric width, cut the pattern in half and cut out eight fabric pieces, joining them up to form four triangles. Position seams centrally on each triangle.

● Pin, tack and stitch the fabric pieces together with plain flat seams into one large square, ending the stitching 5 cm from the centre point. Neaten seams and press open (*fig 3*).

If the room is rectangular, you will have to measure two walls - one long, one short - and make up two different-sized patterns.

● Turn a narrow single hem all round the outer edge; pin, tack and stitch in place.

● Hammer gently on the ceiling to locate the joists if these are not

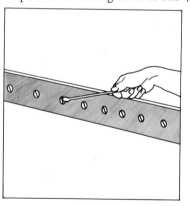

1 Mark and screw the holding battening round the edges of the ceiling.

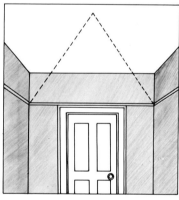

2 Measure from the corner points up to ceiling centre to gauge fabric amounts.

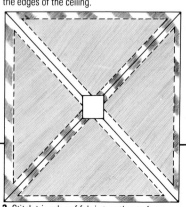

3 Stitch triangles of fabric together to form ceiling of fabric.

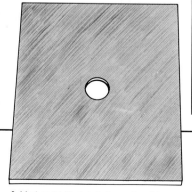

4 Mark and drill a hole in the centre of the plywood.

▲ In this totally fabric-covered room — walls and ceiling — the eye is drawn to their meeting point with short swags of fringed fabric, held at intervals with knots of matching fabric.

already exposed. Measure between the joists and cut a square of plywood to this size. Mark the centre of the plywood and cut a hole large enough to hold the light flex and the fabric (fig 4).

• Turn the raw edges of the centre of the fabric through the hole and secure on the wrong side with fabric adhesive or staples.

• Drill a hole in each corner of the plywood square and screw in place centrally to ceiling, into joists where possible.

• Refix the ceiling rose over the central hole and replace the light fitting and shade.

• At each side, working from the centre, pull the fabric taut at the edges and tack in place to wooden battening. Cover edges of fabric by fixing moulded picture rail over the battening, mitring the corners. Before fixing moulding in place, varnish or paint to match the décor.

Gathered tented ceilings

These obviously require more fabric than ordinary tented ceilings and produce a more lavish effect.

• Mark and fix the battening round the room in the same way as for a plain tented ceiling.

• Make up a pattern in the same way, but cut the triangular pattern in half, adding a rectangle of paper between the two halves. Make the rectangle the same length as the centre line of the triangle and the same width as one half of the triangle. Tape the three pieces together (fig 1).

• From fabric cut out four pieces to this size. It may be necessary to seam two or more fabric widths together to gain the size. If this is the case, position the seams in the same place on each piece. Pin, tack and stitch together with plain flat seams; neaten and press open.

• Turn a double 1.5 cm wide hem/casing round the central hole, leaving an opening at one seam position. Thread a length of fine cord or string round the casing, leaving both ends free at the opening (fig 2). Tie loosely together to hold temporarily.

• Divide the outside edge into equal sections – four or more, depending on size – and work two rows of gathering stitches along each section in turn. Pull up each section in turn and evenly tack in place to the battening.

• At the centre, pull up the gathered centre through a central hole in the plywood as for tented ceilings, covering with a ceiling rose.

• Where there is no central light fitting, mark a circle, 20 cm to 30 cm in diameter, on the square of plywood and tack the gathered fabric to this marked line, pulling up evenly to fit.

• Screw the plywood square in place to the ceiling as before, and cover the gathered centre with fabric-covered thick card. Cut a circle of card, plus a piece of wadding and fabric 2 cm larger all round. Place wadding and then fabric centrally against card and stick raw edges to wrong side (fig 3). Slipstitch circle to ceiling fabric (fig 4). Complete with moulded picture rail as before.

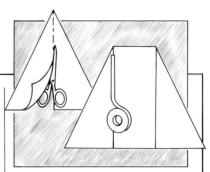

1 Add an extra rectangle in the centre of the pattern and tape together.

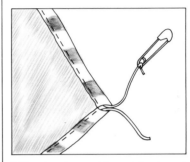

2 Thread a string round the central casing and tie ends loosely together.

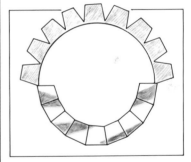

3 Turn excess fabric and wadding over edges of card and stick in place.

4 Slipstitch fabric circle over centre of ceiling to complete the effect.

Loose Covers

Loose covers can be made to fit over most styles of armchair and sofa and, unlike fitted covers, can be removed for cleaning. The fabric must be hard-wearing and able to endure frequent cleaning without shrinking. Firm, tightly-woven fabrics such as a cotton linen mixture, pre-shrunk repp, heavy-duty needlecord, damask or a good quality furnishing cotton are all suitable. Plain colours or small overall patterns are cheaper and easier to work with than large-patterned fabrics, which have to be matched over the chair or sofa.

The best way to make loose covers is to measure each section of the chair and cut out the fabric in rectangles before pin-fitting them, wrong side out, onto the chair. When the fitting is complete, the fabric can be trimmed, the cover removed and the pieces stitched together. Adding covered piping cord between the seams will make the cover more hardwearing, give a tailored look and disguise any failures in pattern matching.

There are many different ways of finishing the base of a sofa or chair, the simplest being a plain, tied-under base. If you opt for a skirt, it is a good idea to decide on the type of skirt before you begin. Choose from a plain skirt with pleated corners, box pleats or a simple gathered skirt, taking into account the style of chair and the décor of the room. The back opening should always be closed with hooks and bars rather than zips which are not strong enough to withstand the wear and tear.

▶ Emphasize the outer edges of a loose cover with matching fabric piping, inserted when the covers are stitched together. Then add piped scatter cushions in toning patterned fabric for a harmonious colour scheme.

▼ An instant solution to a worn-looking sofa is to cover it with an attractive length of fabric. The shaped effect on the arms is created here by clever pleating and invisible stitching.

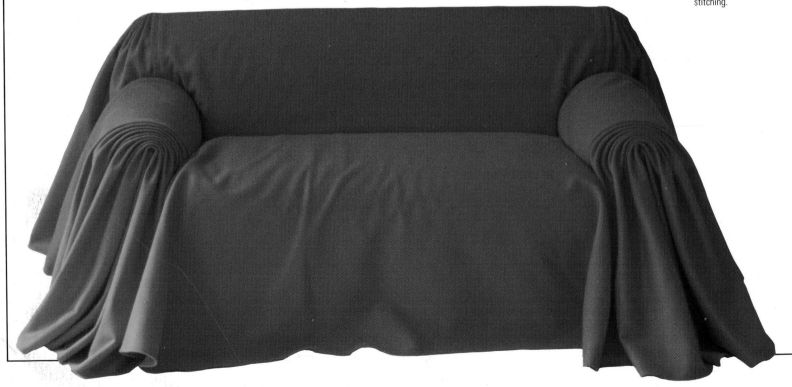

Box shaped loose covers

Good fabrics for loose covers are linen union, repp and heavy-duty needlecord. Keep any left-over scraps of fabric for repairs.

The best method of making loose covers is to measure each section of the sofa/chair at their widest points and cut out rectangles of fabric to size. Then pin-fit these onto the sofa/chair.

● Make a rough diagram of your sofa/chair – a back and a front view – and make a list of the sections to be covered.

● Remove any seat and back cushions and measure each section in turn, marking down the measurements against your list (*fig 1*).

● On a simple box-shaped sofa/ chair the sections will be:
Outside back Length: measure from the top of the back to the base of the sofa/chair. Width: measure across the back at the widest point.
Back box strip Length: measure from top back to top front. Width, measure across the top.
Inside back Length: measure from the top of the inside back down to the point where the back meets the seat. Width: measure across the inside back at the widest point.
Seat Length: measure from meeting point with the inside back to centre of front edge. Width: measure across the seat at the widest point.
Front panel Length: measure from the centre of the front edge to the base. Width: measure from the meeting point with the front arm panel to the opposite side.
Inside arm Length: measure from the top of the arm to meeting point with seat. Width: measure from meeting point with inside back to meeting point with front arm panel.
Arm box strip Length: measure from meeting point with back box strip to

base of sofa. Width: measure from one side to opposite side.
Outside arm Length: measure from meeting point with arm box strip to base of sofa/chair. Width: measure from meeting point with outside back to meeting point with arm box strip.

● Mark in a 5 cm-wide seam allowance both ways on each piece; this will be cut down at the fitting stage, but the size of the allowance will give you some flexibility.

● There needs to be a tuck-in allowance of 15 cm on the length of inside back, inside arms and on the length and width of the seat. This extra fabric is pushed down round the seat to give a taut finish and to hold the cover firmly in place.

● Finally, measure any seat or back cushions both ways, including the gusset pieces.

● Using graph paper, draw your rectangular pattern pieces to scale. Label each piece and cut out.

● On a second sheet of graph paper, mark out your chosen fabric width to the same scale. Place your pattern pieces inside this area, with the grain

lines running in the right direction.

● On patterned fabrics, mark in the pattern repeat and position the pieces accordingly. If there is a particularly large pattern repeat, place the main sections bearing this in mind. Note that the inside arms, outside arms and arm panels should be a mirror image of their opposite numbers (*fig 2*).

● If the cover is to be piped, judge whether there is sufficient fabric left between the pattern pieces to cut the 5 cm-wide bias strips needed to cover the piping cord. If not, add extra for this purpose. The piping will give the seams added strength and make for a more professional look. It is also a good way of disguising the fact if patterned covers do not match exactly at the seams.

As a rough guide, you will need about 12 m of covered cord for a chair and 30 m for a sofa.

● Once the pattern pieces are in place, measure the length that they have taken up and convert back from scale. This will give the required length of fabric.

Cut out the cover pieces as large

1 Draw a rough diagram of your chair and name each section. Make a list adding the measurements of each piece.

2 Draw up each pattern piece to scale and position them on a second sheet of graph paper — marked with the width of the fabric. Place

the pieces in the correct position for grain and pattern matching. Measure the length of pieces taken up for the amount of fabric required

for covering the chair. Remember to add the piping strips if required.

rectangles and then pin-fit them onto the sofa/chair, marking in shaping.
• Place the fabric on the floor and, using a rule and tailors' chalk, mark out each section of the cover.
• As you cut out, identify each piece with a small sticky label, and mark the direction in which the piece should be placed on the sofa/chair. Mark the centre of the outside back, inside back, seat and front border either with a row of pins or with tailors' chalk. Repeat, to mark the centres of the corresponding fabric sections.
• Start by pinning the outside back into position, placing the fabric rectangle wrong side out on the sofa/chair, matching centres.

When using patterned fabric, it might be easier to pin-fit with the right side on the outside, to judge the pattern position, but if you have cut your rectangles accurately, the pattern should fall correctly. If you pin-fit with the right side on the outside, the fabrics will then have to be turned at the stitching stage.
• Smooth the fabric over the sofa/

chair and pin along side edges. Mark round the outside stitching lines with tailors' chalk, using the original upholstery as a guide.
• Position the inside back to the sofa/chair in the same way, remembering the tuck-in allowance at the base. Pin in place. Mark in the seamlines as before. Then pin the back box strip to the sofa/chair in between the outside back and inside back. Pin to both previous pieces and mark in the seamlines.
• Pin the outside arms, then inside arms to the sofa/chair in the same way, adding the arm box strips. Pin arm box strips to back box strip and then outside arm to outside back down outside edge of sofa/chair.
• Matching centre marks, pin seat in place, leaving the tuck-in allowance free at the back and at each side. Match and pin the tuck-in allowances together round the seat to inside back and inside arms. Match and pin front panel to seat and arm pieces (fig 3).
• Carefully remove the cover from the sofa; tack and stitch together in the same order in which it was

pinned together. Trim and zigzag stitch the raw edges as you work.
• Leave one outside back/outside arm edge open for about three-quarters its length for the opening.
• All the seams that outline the sofa/chair can be piped. Piping should be inserted between the pieces when they are stitched together. Snip up to the stitching at top of the opening.
• Face the back opening: cut a strip of matching fabric, twice the length of the opening and 8 cm wide. Pin, tack and stitch this strip with right sides together to the wrong side of the opening. Turn in 1.5 cm along raw edge of strip and place over raw edge of cover to previous stitching line. Stitch in place. Fold strip in half and to the inside of the cover.
• Place cover over the sofa/chair and check for fit.
• Stitch hook and eye fastenings on either side of the opening (fig 4).
• For a plain tied-under finish, measure the underside of the sofa/chair base to find the position of the castors/feet.
• From matching fabric cut out four

pieces to the length of the skirt sides and 18 cm wide. Place against the sofa/chair base and mark in the angles of the corners. Cut off excess fabric to fit.
• Pin, tack and stitch 1 cm-wide double hems along all side edges of each flap piece.
• Turn a double 3 cm-hem/casing to the wrong side along inside edges of each flap piece. Pin, tack and stitch in place.
• Place flaps against cover with right sides together, matching corner points. Pin, tack and stitch together. Zigzag stitch raw edges to neaten.
• Cut a single length of 1 cm-wide cotton tape to fit round base of sofa/chair. Using a safety pin, thread one end through all the casings in turn, beginning at open back edges.
• Place cover over sofa/chair, fitting into place. Pull up tape until cover fits securely in place. Tie tape into a bow and tuck up at the tied corner (fig 5).

Alternative skirt finishes

Tailored skirt with corner pleats
Place the cover over the sofa/chair and mark round the base 13.5 cm from floor. Trim off excess fabric.
• Measure the sofa/chair and cut a piece of fabric the length of each section, plus seam allowances by 18 cm deep.
• Cut out an insert for each corner, 18 cm square. Pin, tack and stitch skirt

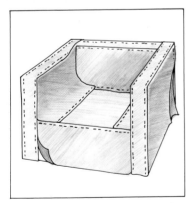

3 Pin-fit the fabric rectangles onto the chair, positioning the extra tuck-in allowance all round the seat.

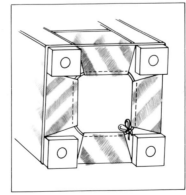

4 To hold the cover on the chair, stitch hook and eye fastenings into the faced back opening.

5 Pull up cotton tape, till cover is stretched firmly over the chair. Tie into a bow and push inside the cover.

▲ Contrasting piped edges highlight the clean-cut lines of this two-seated sofa. Make up a plain skirt with inverted corner pleats and top with patterned scatter cushions piped in the same fabric as the sofa.

▶ Clever positioning of this unusual fabric ensures that the pattern matches across all the separate sections of the chair. The whole seat is outlined with self-fabric piping cord.

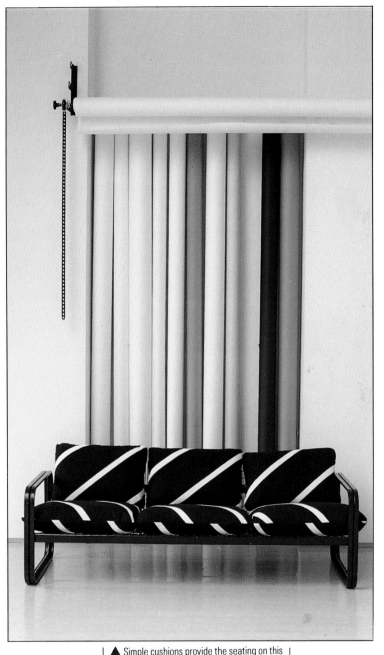

▲ Simple cushions provide the seating on this modern tubular sofa. Use striped fabric positioned at an angle round the back and seat cushions to give the illusion of spirals.

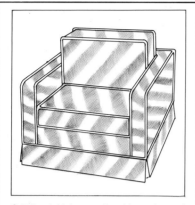

6 Tailored: Make up a skirt with neat inverted pleats at each corner.

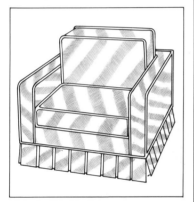

7 Pleated: Pleat the skirt up from the centre so uneven pleats will be at back opening.

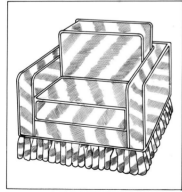

8 Gathered: Gather up each section of the skirt and match to each section of the chair.

pieces with right sides together in order; outside back, inset, outside arm, inset, front, inset, outside arm, inset. Turn and stitch a double 2.5 cm wide hem down each open edge of skirt.

• Pin, tack and stitch a single 2.5 cm wide hem all round the skirt. Fold each section to meet centrally over inset to form an inverted pleat at each corner. Pin and tack across raw top edge to hold.

• Pin, tack and stitch skirt to the cover, neatening raw edges with zig-zag stitch.

• Add extra fastenings into opening as for main cover (fig 6).

Pleated skirt Mark the lower edge of the cover in the same way as for a tailored skirt. Decide on the size of the box pleats and cut and stitch 18 cm-long strips together to make up into one continuous length of the required size.

• At each short edge, turn under a double 2.5 cm-wide hem and stitch.

• Turn up a 2.5 cm-wide single hem; pin, tack and stitch in place. Fold up the skirt into even pleats, beginning at the centre of the strip and working both ways. In this way an uneven pleat will be positioned at the opening edge where it will be inconspicuous. Press and tack skirt along raw top edge.

• Place skirt against cover with right sides together, matching skirt ends to back opening edges. Pin, tack and stitch in place.

• Add extra fastenings as for main cover (fig 7).

Gathered skirt Measure and make up a skirt strip as for the pleated skirt, one and a half times the total distance round the sofa/chair.

• Stitch side and base hems.

• Divide the skirt into four and

work two rows of gathering stitches round top raw edge of each section.

• Place skirt with right side against cover, matching opening edges. Pull up gathering stitches evenly in each section in turn to match each section of the sofa/chair. Pin, tack and stitch skirt in place, neatening edges with zigzag stitch.

• Add extra fastenings as for main cover (fig 8).

Shaped loose covers

When making up loose covers for shaped sofas/chairs, the principles and methods are the same as for box-shaped loose covers, if a little more complicated. The shaped back and arms have to be fitted more carefully before stitching together.

• Measure up the sofa/chair in the same way as before, remembering always to measure across the widest part of each section.

When measuring a shaped sofa/chair, the outside and inside back sections will stitch together without a back box strip, and similarly there will be no arm box strips. The seam on the arm top – which divides the inside arm from the outside arm – will have to be positioned.

• Either follow the lines of the original upholstery or mark where the seam will fall – halfway round the scroll on the outside is a good position – onto the sofa/chair with a row of pins. There will be a front arm panel that will also be shaped at the pinning stage.

• When pin-fitting the cover onto the sofa/chair, the top seam of the inside back will have to be pleated up to remove the excess fabric formed by the curved shape (fig 1). Rather than take a large pleat, make a series of small pleats equally placed at each side of the sofa/chair back. There may be fullness that needs to be removed round the top of the front arm panels and this can be

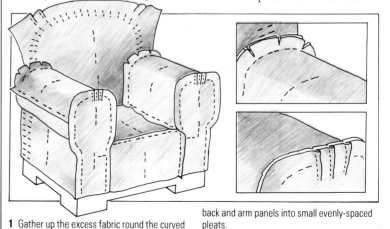

1 Gather up the excess fabric round the curved back and arm panels into small evenly-spaced pleats.

pleated out as for the back.

• When dealing with the arm sections, snip into the inside back section at each side so it will wrap round the arm, trim carefully so there will be a normal seam allowance at the top but a full tuck-in allowance at the seat. Trim the inside arm in the same way to match. Clip into the allowance round the top of the arm to gain a smooth fit.

Piped gusseted cushions

To make a loose cover for a sofa/chair cushion, you will need a strong zip for the back opening.

• Measure the cushion pad both ways and cut out two pieces of fabric to this size, plus 3 cm seam allowance.

The gusset is divided up into four sections: the back which extends round both back corners for 8 cm to give a wider opening; two side pieces the length of the cushion pad minus 8 cm; and one front piece the length of the cushion pad front.

• Add 3 cm to all measurements for seam allowance. Measure gusset depth adding seam allowance as before. Add an extra 3 cm seam allowance to the back gusset width to allow for the central zip opening.

• Measure and cut out each piece. Then cut the back gusset in half lengthways.

• Turn in central raw edges for 1.5 cm on back gusset; pin and tack. Place a zip centrally behind the folded edges. Pin, tack and stitch zip in place. Stitch across the gusset at either end of zip (fig 1).

• Cut out 5 cm-wide bias strips and make up sufficient covered piping to fit twice round the cushion. Place covered piping round outer edge of cushion top. Pin, tack and stitch piping in place, joining together at position of one back seam to fit. Repeat to stitch covered piping round cushion base in the same way.

• Pin, tack and stitch side gusset pieces to either end of front gusset

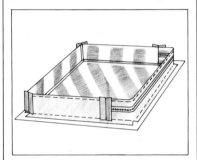

1 Position seams carefully to allow for a large opening at the back.

piece, beginning and ending stitching 1.5 cm from outer edges; this allows the gusset to split open at the corners when stitched to cushion top and base. Stitch back gusset to either end of side gusset pieces in the same way to complete gusset ring.

• Place gusset against top cushion piece with right sides together, matching front gusset seams to front corners. Pin, tack and stitch

• Open zip, stitch base edge of gusset to cushion base in same way.

• Trim and turn cushion cover to the right side through the zip. Insert cushion pad and close zip.

1 The white edging of the loose, removable quilted cover lends dramatic effect.

2 The piped cushion covers here echo the style of the sofa's fitted cover.

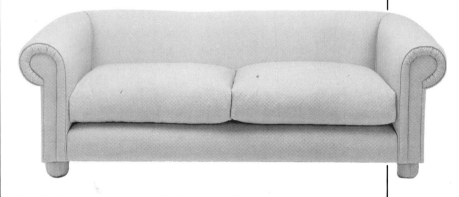

3 The sofa's hard piped edge contrasts with the seamless cushions.

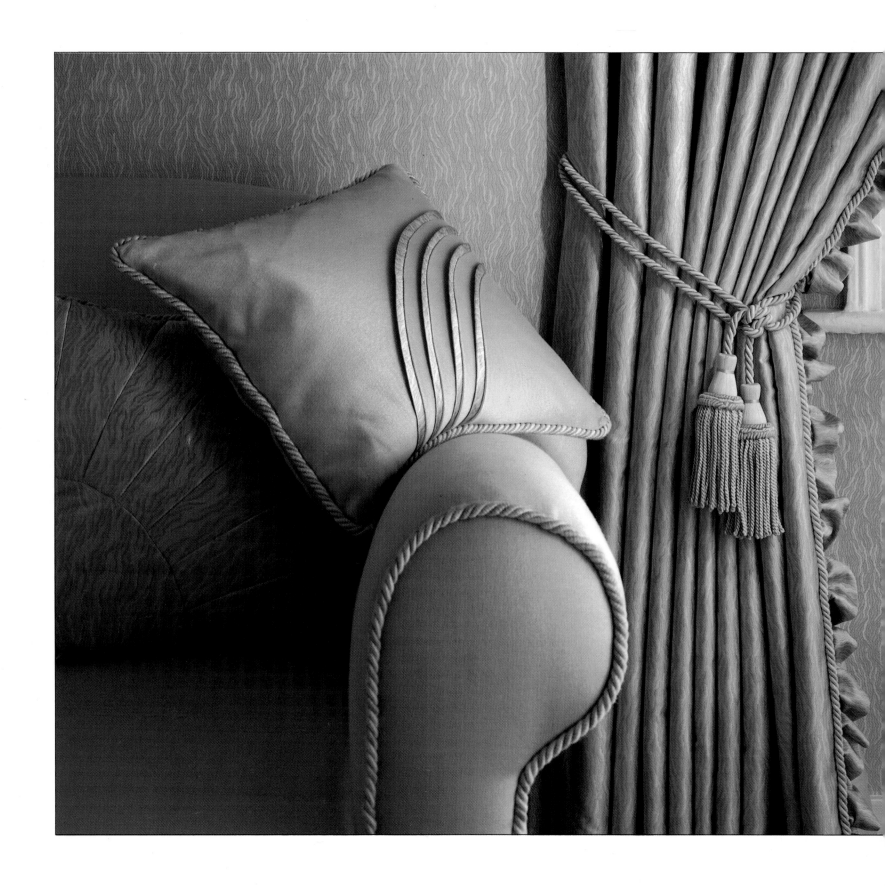

Cushions

◄ Beautifully seamed cushions show how a simple shape can be turned into an important feature in a room. The cushion has curved bands of flat piping inserted into the plain front. Once made, the whole shape benefits from the addition of a twisted cord edge, echoing the loose covers and curtains.

▼ You can give large seat cushions a lift by cutting the gusset from the fabric length and adding plain piping around the top and bottom edges. By echoing the same colour piping round the patterned scatter cushions, a modern decor can be brought to life.

As well as adding the finishing touches to sofas, beds and chairs, cushions can even provide basic seating units by themselves. Small scatter cushions can give extra comfort in an armchair or add a touch of colour to a plain three-piece suite. They can be made in any shape or size: square, round, oval, heart-shaped, or they can be bolster-shaped to provide arms for a sofa or a headrest for a bed.

The choice of fabric for cushions will depend on the cushion's function. Heavy-duty fabrics are suitable for loose covers and floor cushions; general furnishing fabrics for scatter cushions; while lace and delicate fabrics can be used on cushions that are purely decorative. Off-cuts from curtains or bedspreads can easily be used to make up cushion covers, with any spare lining fabric for the cushion pad. If the fabric off-cuts are too small, combine them with other similar fabrics to make up patchwork or appliqué covers.

Always use a cushion pad and make sure that the cushion pad cover is made up in a fabric compatible with the filling; thus a feather and down filling must be teamed with a downproof fabric, while plain cotton, calico or lining fabrics are suitable covers for synthetic fillings.

There are many different ways to close a cushion cover, the simplest is to slipstich the opening (the stitches can be removed when the cover is washed and it does not take long to stitch it up again). Alternative fastenings are: zips, touch and close fastenings, press fasteners – individual ones or rows of them on a tape – plain ties, or buttons with holes or loops.

Decorative edgings may be added, such as covered piping, a single or double frill in self or contrasting fabric, or a lace or broderie anglaise trim. Square cushion covers can also have the addition of a flat border, while bolsters may have gathered ends with tassels or covered buttons.

Cushion pads

Always marry the filling of the cushion pad with the fabric of the outer cover; for instance, a feather and down filling requires a cover made of feather-proof cambric.

- Make up the cushion pad to match the cushion cover, omitting any form of fastening and trimming. Cut out two pieces to the required size plus 3 cm all round for seam allowance.
- Place covers with right sides together; pin, tack and stitch together all round with two rows of stitching for strength, and leave an opening of at least 20 cm centrally in one side.
- Trim and turn to right side. Fill firmly; turn in opening edges in line with the seam and slipstitch to close, taking small stitches.

Square cushion covers

Basic square cushion covers are quick and easy to make.

- From fabric cut out two pieces to the required size, allowing for 1.5 cm seam allowance.
- Place fabric pieces with right sides together, pin, tack and stitch together all round, leaving an opening centrally in one side.
- Trim down the seam allowance to 1 cm cutting across corner points. Neaten all round with zigzag stitching. Turn cover to the right side.
- Insert cushion pad. Turn in opening edges in line with the remainder of the seam. Pin, tack and slipstitch with small, neat stitches.

If you want to be able to remove your cushion cover for laundering without unpicking the stitches each time, there are various alternative methods of fastening the opening:

1 For a zip fastening, place fabric pieces with right sides together; pin and tack together all along one side. Stitch in from each side, leaving a central opening. Place the zip right side down on the seam allowances over the tacked part of the seam. Pin, tack and stitch zip in place from the right side. Finish making up cushion as before.

If the cushion has a distinctive front, the zip can be inserted across the back of the cushion. Add 3 cm to back piece to allow for opening.

2 Touch and close fastening, spots, single press fasteners or press fastening tape and hooks and bars can be added in two ways. Either stitch these fastenings to the seam allowances on either side of the opening, snipping into the allowance up to the stitching on one side of the opening so the fastenings can fasten together neatly. Or, make a double hem on one side of the cover, then stitch alongside to provide a substantial base for the fastenings, in the same way as for a duvet cover (see page 129).

▼ A window seat can be brought to life with cushions — here the seat itself is covered with a deep-gusseted foam cushion, shaped to fit the bay. The fabric is matched to the blinds hanging above the seat. Frilled square scatter cushions with a row of piping inserted between the frill and cushion provide a finishing touch.

▶ Simple, plain-edged scatter cushions in a variety of plain and patterned fabrics add to the comfort of the seating units. Choose matching fabrics and then pick one plain colour from the fabric to add touches of colour around the room.

Round cushion covers

- To make a circular paper pattern, cut out a square of paper, slightly larger than your intended circle. Fold the paper in half both ways.
- Cut a length of string 15 cm longer than the circle radius. Fasten a drawing pin through one end of the string into the folded corner of the paper.
- Tie the opposite end of the string round the pointed end of a pencil with string the length of desired radius. Draw an arc from one side of the paper to the other. Keeping the paper folded, cut along the marked

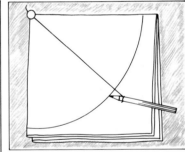

1 Fold paper in half both ways. Draw an arc from one side to the other.

line. Unfold paper.
- Using this pattern cut out two pieces from fabric adding 1.5 cm seam allowance all round. Place with right sides together: pin, tack and stitch together all round, leaving an opening for turning. Trim and turn to right side. Insert cushion pad. Turn in opening edges in line with the remainder of the seam. Insert zip, or other method of fastening described above, or slipstitch opening edges.
- To add a double frill to a round cushion cover, measure the circum-

ference of the cushion cover and double the measurement. Cut out sufficient fabric strips to make up this length by the desired width. Pin, tack and stitch strips together into a ring with plain flat seams.
- Fold frill in half with wrong sides together. Divide up into four equal sections and work two rows of gathering stitches in each section. Divide up outer edge of cover into four. Place frill against right side of one cover piece pulling up gathers evenly to fit each section. Pin and tack. Place second cover piece with right side to first and make up as before.

Plain bolster covers

Traditionally used to bolster pillows on a bed, bolster cushions are long and sausage-shaped.
- Decide on the diameter you require and make up a circular pattern for the bolster ends in the same way as for the round cushion cover. Measure round the outer edge of the pattern for the width of the main cover piece.
- Cut out one piece of fabric to this size by the desired length, remembering to add 1.5 cm seam allowance all round. Cut out two end circles. Fold the main piece in half with right sides together, raw edges matching.
- Pin, tack and stitch in from each side, leaving a central opening for zip

(*fig 1*). Press seam open.
- Position the zip behind opening edges. Pin, tack and stitch zip in place (*fig 2*). Open zip.
- Snip into seam allowance all round circular end pieces (*fig 3*).
- With wrong sides together, pin, tack and stitch circular end pieces into each end of the bolster. Trim and turn to right side through zip.
- Insert cushion pad; close zip.

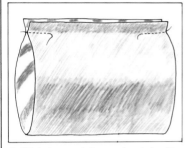

1 Stitch the seam in from each end of cushion, leaving opening for zip.

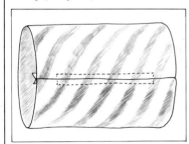

2 Pin, tack and stitch zip behind the central opening in seam.

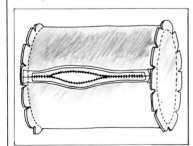

3 Snip into seam allowance round ends, then stitch to main piece.

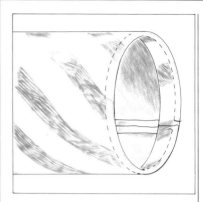

1 Work a row of gathering round end of cover. Place pad centrally inside.

2 Pull up gathering stitches and bring edges together. Fasten off.

3 Place a tassel with embellished base over gathered end. Stitch in place.

Gathered bolster covers

These are slightly more elaborate than plain bolster covers – the gathering is added for decoration. This kind of bolster is particularly well suited to the end of a sofa rather than bolstering pillows at a bedhead, where its decorative ends may be obscured, and the cover can be made to match or tone with the sofa.

• Measure the length of the bolster pad and add the diameter of the circular end plus 3 cm seam allowance. Measure the circumference and add 3 cm for the width.

• Cut out one piece of fabric to this size. Fold fabric with right sides together, long edges matching. Pin and tack and then stitch along the raw edges.

• Turn cover to the right side. Turn in 1.5 cm to wrong side at each end. Pin and tack.

• Work a row of gathering stitches round each turned-in end, close to folded edge.

• Place bolster cushion pad centrally inside cover (*fig 1*).

• Pull up gathering stitches at each end of cover to bring the edges together and fasten off gathering thread. Repeat at the opposite end (*fig 2*).

• Stitch a tassel to each end, with the rosette covering the gathered end (*fig 3*).

▲ Here the metallic feel of the wallcoverings is reflected in the collection of scatter cushions in shiny fabrics.

Shaped kitchen chair cushions

Also known as squab cushions, these are designed to fit and tie onto a straight chair and can be matched to other furnishings.

- Cut a piece of paper to fit the seat. Place on the seat, mark round the outline and cut out pattern.
- Place pattern on chair seat to check for fit and mark in positions of fastening ties.
- Place pattern on fabric and cut out twice, adding 1.5 cm seam allowance all round.
- For ties, cut out two straight fabric pieces 60 cm by 5 cm. Press in 1 cm along each long edge to centre. Press in 5 mm at each end. Fold tie in half. Pin, tack and stitch all round tie. Repeat to make up second tie in the same way.
- Make up two lengths of piping each long enough to fit round cushion. Place covered piping round each cushion piece, snipping into fabric at curves and corners. Join piping fabric together to fit centrally in back edge.
- Fold each tie in half and place folded ends to raw edge of cover at marked points. Pin (fig 1).
- Cut out one 4 cm-wide gusset strip that will fit from back corner round to opposite back corner, and one back gusset strip. Pin, tack and stitch gusset strips together into a ring, beginning and ending stitching 1.5 cm from either end of seam.
- Pin, tack and stitch one edge of gusset to one side of cushion piece over piping, matching seams to back corners. Pin, tack and stitch remaining edge of gusset to second cushion piece, leaving an opening in between fastening ties, at the centre back. Trim and turn to the right side.
- Place pattern on 4 cm-thick foam and mark round. Cut out foam shape. Insert foam into cover. Turn in opening edges in line with the remainder of the seam and slipstitch together to close.
- As an alternative method of fastening cushion to chair, use elasticated fabric loops and small toggles positioned in the same place at the back of the cushion.

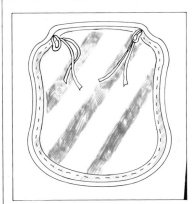

1. Place the centre of each tie to marked positions at the back corners.

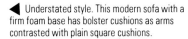

◀ Understated style. This modern sofa with a firm foam base has bolster cushions as arms contrasted with plain square cushions.

Fixed Upholstery

◀ Fixed furnishing is a risky business. The fabic you choose must be able to resist wear, tear and stains. You can't take them off for cleaning. Dining-chairs are particularly vulnerable. But something dark and non-absorbent should stay the course.

▼ Few essential tools are needed for upholstery. It is best however, to start with a small hammer, tacks, curved needles and a webbing strainer.

An upholstered chair or sofa has a cover that is permanently nailed in place and cannot be removed for cleaning. Because of this, be careful in your choice of fabric for the top cover – it will need to be hard-wearing and reasonably stain-proof. Dralon velvet is a popular choice.

Upholstery can be worked using either foam as the padding or the more traditional horsehair or fibre. The old-fashioned upholstery will generally last longer than the modern foam, which will start to deteriorate after about five years.

Simple pin-seats or drop-in seats can be speedily upholstered with a layer of foam over webbing, and easy-to-obtain fabrics such as calico and hessian. The only really essential tools are a small or upholsterers' hammer and a block of wood or webbing strainer for tightening the webbing base on which the seat rests. For a sprung seat, coiled springs and a suitable fibre filling are also necessary. Previously, horsehair was used, but this has now been supplanted by fibre mixture.

You may find complete re-seating unnecessary and that once the top cover has been removed, all that needs to be done is to top up the filling and make a new top cover. The bottoming and webbing can also be renewed without disturbing the remainder of the chair. Partial re-upholstery, such as the simple job of replacing buttons on a buttoned seat, will often be all that is needed to give a chair a new lease of life.

However, if the chair needs a completely new look, once the old materials have been stripped away, check the woodwork for damage and woodworm and treat it before the cover is replaced. The frame can also be cleaned and re-stained.

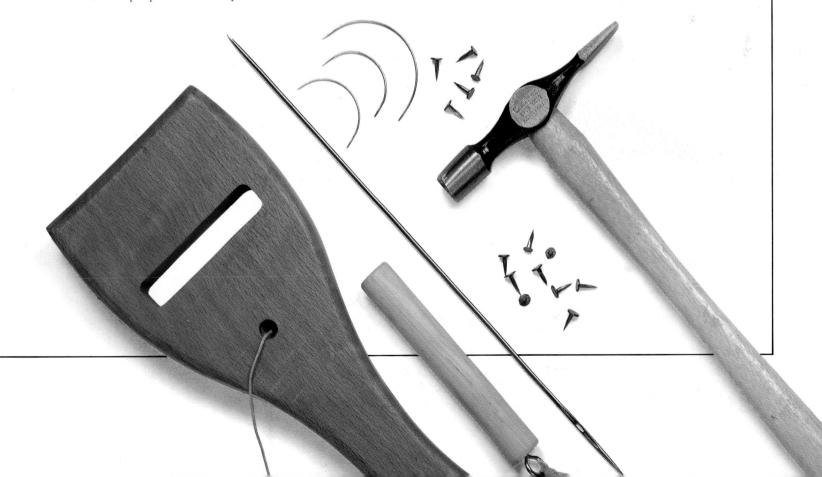

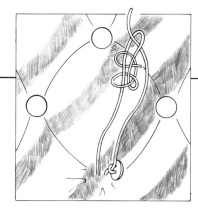

1. Push needle back through the padding, making a loop of twine.

2 Knot ends together with a slip knot and pull tight.

Replacing buttons

Always replace all the covered buttons at the same time, so they will match. Choose button moulds the same size as the original buttons and cover with the same fabric or one of similar weight, following the manufacturers' instructions.

• Thread a double-pointed upholsterers' needle with strong twine. Insert the unthreaded end at first button point and push through the padding till point emerges on the opposite side.

• When the eye is visible, push the needle back through the padding till it emerges 6 mm from where it first entered, making a loop of twine inside the padding (*fig 1*).

• Unthread the needle. Thread the button shank onto to one end of the twine. Tie to the other end with a slip knot (*fig 2*). Pull the knot tight until the button sinks into the padding. Knot the two lengths together and trim off ends.

• Repeat with each button, making sure that each one is pulled into the padding by the same amount.

Upholstering a drop in seat

Foam, combined with strong webbing, hessian, hard-wearing lining fabric and calico, makes a very sturdy seat.

• Place a layer of newspaper under the chair and strip off the old materials using a ripping chisel and mallet to remove the tacks. Clean the frame, stripping and re-varnishing if necessary and filling in any large holes.

• Position evenly-spaced rows of webbing across the seat frame both ways with the spaces in between each length and the frame no wider than the webbing.

• On a small seat place at least two rows of webbing both ways; on a larger seat place three or more rows. If the seat front is wider than the back, fan out each strand of webbing slightly to accommodate the extra width.

• Working from the roll, turn under 2.5 cm of webbing and place on top of the back frame, about 1.5 cm in from the back edge.

• Hammer webbing in place with five tacks in a W shape – three tacks at the back and two in front positioned in the two gaps (*fig 1*).

• Either using a webbing strainer or by wrapping the webbing round a short length of wood, pull the webbing taut over the seat frame to front edge. Holding it taut, hammer three tacks in place (*fig 2*).

• Cut off the excess webbing 2.5 cm from tacks. Fold back excess and hammer in two more tacks to form the W shape as before.

• Repeat for each length of webbing working first from back to front, then from side to side, weaving the webbing under and over the first set before fixing in place.

• Cut out a piece of hessian on the straight of grain to cover the webbing. Measure the seat for size adding 1 cm all round.

• Place the hessian centrally on seat frame over webbing, with the grain running parallel to the seat frame. Turn up the raw edge and tack to the frame through folded edge, placing tacks between 5 mm and 1 cm from outer edge. At each corner, fold hessian into a neat fold (*fig 3*).

• Cut out a piece of 5 cm-thick foam, 1.3 cm larger all round than the seat frame.

• Trim the edges of the foam by cutting a triangular-shape strip from the bottom edges (*fig 4*).

▲ Reupholstering both the back and the drop in seat in the same colour can be very attractive.

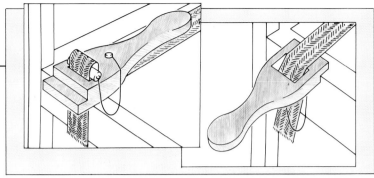

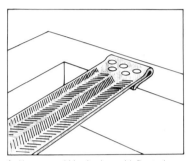

1 Hammer webbing in place with five tacks forming a W shape.

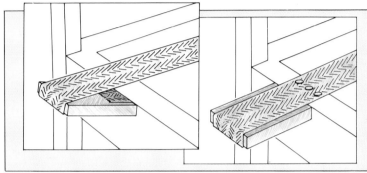

2 With webbing strainer, pull webbing taut over seat frame to front edge.

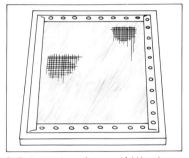

3 Tack raw edge to frame and fold hessian into a neat fold at corners.

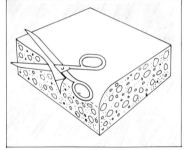

4 Trim foam by cutting a triangular-shape strip from the bottom edges.

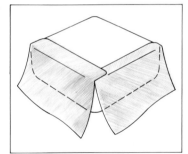

5 Stick fabric strips to edges of foam with fabric adhesive, overlapping at corners.

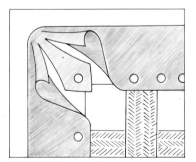

6 Pull the fabric over the corner and tack the central tongue.

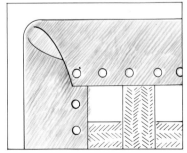

7 Cut out the excess fabric in the pleat and tack over the central fixing.

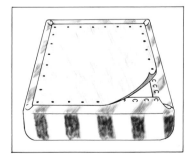

8 Tack a top cover over the bottom of the seat frame in the same way.

- Cut out a strip of calico for each side of the foam (each strip should be 10 cm wide by the length of the side, plus 15 cm.
- Stick each fabric strip in turn to the edges of the foam with fabric adhesive. Place centrally on the foam and stick half the width on the top, overlapping the strips at each corner. Leave to dry thoroughly (*fig 5*).
- Place the foam centrally on the seat, feathered side down.
- Turn the frame over and pull the strips over the edge to the underside and half-tack (temporarily) each side in place. Adjust and tighten the tacks, pulling down evenly all round. Trim the strips at the corners and pull down each corner, folding the excess fabric into small pleats.
- Cut out a piece of heavyweight cotton lining the same size as the frame, on the straight of grain, adding 10 cm all round.
- Place lining centrally over the foam on top of the seat and tack to the underside, smoothing over the foam and pulling it down at the same time to achieve a rounded shape. At each corner, pull the fabric over the seat and tack (*fig 6*).
- Fold in two side pleats towards the centre tack, cutting out excess fabric from underneath the pleat. Tack in place (*fig 7*).
- Cut out and tack top cover to the seat frame in the same way as the lining.
- Cut out a piece of hessian on the straight of grain, the same size as the underside of the seat frame. Place hessian centrally to the underside of the seat frame. Turn under edges evenly all round and tack in place over raw edges of fabric and lining (*fig 8*).
- Replace seat in chair.

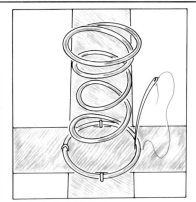

1 Stitch the base of each spring to the webbing with a half-circular needle.

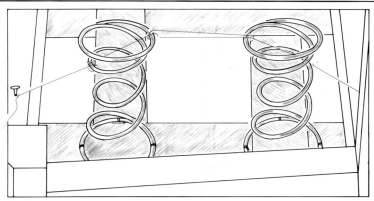

2 Take the twine through the spring and loop round the top coil on the opposite side.

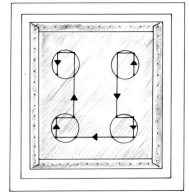

3 Stitch tops of springs to the hessian using a curved needle.

4 At back corners, turn back the calico and cut out corner to within 1 cm of fold.

Upholstering a sprung seat

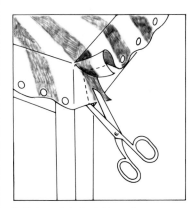

5 Make neat pleats at sides and corners, matching edges of seat.

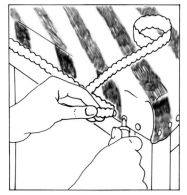

6 Cover raw fabric edges and tacks with decorative braid.

A chair that is upholstered with jute-webbing, springs and horsehair or fibre should last for years. You will need a half-circular needle, a curved needle and a double-pointed needle. You may find you are able to re-use the original springs and horsehair or fibre filling. In addition, you will need scrim, wadding, calico and decorative braid.

• Strip off and prepare the chair in the same way as for a drop-in seat. Replace the webbing in the same way as for a drop-in seat, but position on the underside of the frame.

• Turn the chair upright.

• Position the springs on the webbing intersections

• Stitch the base of each spring to the webbing, using twine and a half-circular needle. Work three stitches on each side, forming a square (beginning each set with a slip knot). Pass on to the next spring and repeat until all the springs have been attached to the webbing in the same way. Fasten off firmly (*fig 1*).

• Lash down the springs: hammer a tack half-way into the top of the seat frame centrally in line with each spring. Make a slip knot in a long length of twine, leaving about 20 cm free, and loop over the tack at the back of the frame. Pull the knot tight and hammer in the tack. Depress the first spring in front of the tack to two-thirds its height and loop the twine round the second coil on the first spring. Take the twine through the spring and loop round the top coil on the opposite side (*fig 2*).

• Carry over to the next spring and while keeping it depressed, loop the twine round the top coil. Take twine through spring to the opposite side and round the second coil. Finally, knot twine round the half-depressed tack in the front seat frame and hammer into frame.

• Repeat with second row of springs. Then work in the same way from side to side across the seat.

• Knot the long length of twine left free at each outside edge back to the top coil of each spring.

• Place hessian centrally over seat and cut out roughly to size, adding 2.5 cm all round.

• Fold back the raw edges of hessian and tack to the top of the frame through the folded edge. Trim off excess fabric as you work.

• Stitch the tops of the springs to the hessian using a curved needle in the same way as when stitching them to

▲ The finished article — a recently recovered sprung chair, showing how effective such renovation can be. Here the padded back of the chair has been re-upholstered using a similar technique.

the webbing. beginning and ending with a slip knot as shown (*fig 3*).

● Make bridle ties to hold the filling in place: thread a length of twine onto a half-circular needle. Secure at the right-hand front corner about 8 cm from edges with a slip knot.

● Work round the seat. making a series of large back stitches, leaving loops in between large enough to slide in a flattened hand. Fasten off.

● Tease out the fibre and force handfuls under the bridle ties. Then fill in the centre of the seat until it is about 15 cm deep.

● Place scrim centrally over filling and roughly cut to size, adding 2.5 cm all round the outer edge. Turn under the outer edge for at least 2.5 cm and temporarily tack to all four sides to hold in place. Then, smoothing over the seat, tack in place, trimming off excess as you work round seat.

● Using a long needle and twine, stitch round the seat through all layers with large tacking stitches, about 7 cm from outer edge, ending in the centre.

● With a double-pointed needle, work blind stitching round the edge of the seat to give it a firm edge. Begin 2.5 cm from corner strut. Insert the needle at a 45° angle just above the tacks to reappear 5 cm up from the edge. Push the needle back, making it reappear slightly to the left. Make a slip knot and pull tight.

● Insert the needle again 5 cm to the right of this stitch and knot as before. Continue round the seat edge.

● To make a firm edge, mark two guidelines about 2.5 cm apart on both sides of the seat edge. Pinch together and stitch from the back of the seat. Insert the needle through the lower guideline so it emerges through the upper guideline. Pull

through and reinsert on the upper line slightly to the left of the first stitch. Secure with a slip knot. Insert the needle 2.5 cm to the right of the knot and pull out on the upper line.

● Insert the needle again on the upper line halfway between the knot and the stitch. Pull through, wrapping the twine round the needle. Continue in this way round the edge of the seat.

● Cut out a piece of medium-weight wadding slightly larger than the seat top placed over the scrim.

● Cut out a piece of calico 5 cm larger than the seat all round, on the straight of grain. Place calico centrally over the wadding and temporarily hold in place on each side.

● Tack in place to the sides of the frame, trimming off excess fabric as you work. At the front corners, make an inverted pleat, trimming away excess fabric from behind.

● At the back corners, turn back the calico and cut out the corner to within 1 cm of fold. Fold back and take the calico round the strut (*fig 4*).

● Cut out and place another layer of wadding over the calico. With the grain straight and centralizing any pattern, cut out a piece of top cover fabric to the same size as the calico. Place centrally over the seat, and tack.

● At the front corners, take the front fabric round and tack to the sides. then bring the side fabric over the top, making a neat pleat with the fold matching the edge. Tack (*fig 5*).

● Stick a length of decorative braid round the side of the seat using fabric adhesive and, covering raw fabric edges and tacks. Turn under the raw edge at each side (*fig 6*).

● Turn the chair over and apply hessian to the underside as for the drop-in seat, working round each leg.

Bedrooms

Bedrooms are the most intimate rooms in the house. They are where you dream and where dreams come true. They are intensely personal, for it is here that you show a side of yourself that few in the outside world will ever see.

▶ Restful colours and soft shapes are not the only option for bedrooms. They can be jazzy. It's just a matter of tailoring your approach to your personality.

Bed Linen

Decidedly feminine, this bedroom is beautifully decorated with white bed linen. Frilled pillowcases match up with the edge of the throw-over bedspread that has the addition of white ribbon bows.

With wide-width sheeting now readily available, making bedlinen is easy. And, when making duvet covers, there is the added advantage of being able to mix and match the fabrics to suit the bedroom décor. You can produce exactly the look you want, and be almost certain that it's unique!

Sheeting fabric is not essential for pillowcases; just check that the fabric of your choice can be washed frequently without shrinking or changing colour. A bed can look particularly attractive with totally contrasting pillowcases or with pillowcases edged with frills of broderie anglaise or similar fabric.

Duvets provide as much warmth as the combind forces of blankets and eiderdowns, but they are expensive to buy, so making one is economically viable. Basically, a duvet is a bag divided up into walled channels into which the chosen filling is stuffed. There are various types of filling: natural fillings such as feather and down mixtures and synthetic fillings that have the advantage of being washable so are ideal for children, as well as for people who are allergic to feather. The outer cover of the duvet must be compatible with the filling – use a downproof cambric, shiny side inside for natural-mix fillings, while a plain cotton sheeting is suitable for covering a synethetic filling.

Duvet covers should be the same size as the duvet and have a large central opening in the base edge of the cover. This opening can be fastened with a length of press fastening tape, touch and close fastening, individual press fasteners, buttons and buttonholes, or just simple ties.

Because they do not need to be laundered as often as sheets and duvet covers, bed valances need not be made in sheeting fabric, a contrasting fabric may be preferred.

Valances, bedspreads and divan covers can be finished in a variety of ways – the flounce can be straight, have corner pleats, box pleats, knife pleats or gathers. Bedspreads and divan covers will look more tailored if the main pieces are outlined with a covered piping cord or with a plain bias binding in a matching or contrasting shade. If the bedspread fabric has sufficient weight it will not need a lining – simply stitch any seams as flat fell seams and stitch double hems all round the outer edge. Braid trims and edgings can be added to give the bedspread an individual look.

▲ Vibrant colours liven up this set of bed linen. Mix and match similar fabrics for pillowcases, sheets and quilted bedspread.

Flat sheets

The most practical fabric for sheets is wide-width cotton or cotton/polyester.

● Measure the mattress both ways and add twice the depth and 25cm. tuck-under allowance, then cut out the fabric to this size. adding 21 cm to the length and 4 cm to the width for

1 Thread a length of cord through a channel of stitching.

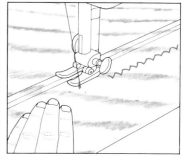

2 Hold cord down and zigzag stitch in position along the sheet hem.

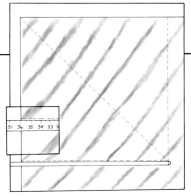

hems. Turn under a double 1 cm hem down each side edge. Pin, tack and stitch side hems in place. At the base edge, turn under a double 2.5 cm-wide hem; pin, tack and stitch in place. At the top edge, turn under a double 8 cm-wide hem; pin and tack.

● To make a corded hem along the top edge of the sheet, with a straight-stitching sewing-machine, stitch along the hem 1 cm in from the inner fold. Stitch along the hem again 1.3 cm from fold. Using a fine tapestry needle, thread a length of fine cord through the casing formed by the stitching (*fig 1*). Fasten each end in place.

● On a swing-needle sewing-machine, simply place the cord along the hem and zigzag-stitch over the cord to hold it in place (*fig 2*).

Fitted sheets

These need to be measured very accurately. The gathered corners are made with household elastic.

● Measure the bed top both ways and to both measurements add twice the mattress depth plus twice the 18 cm tuck-in allowance.

● From the fabric, cut out one piece of this size.

● Make each gathered corner as follows: measure 36 cm along from each side of corner point and mark. Measure in at right angles from these two marks until they meet and mark

1 Mark out the corner dart matching the two outer points together.

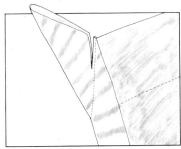

2 Stitch the dart at each corner with a French seam for durability.

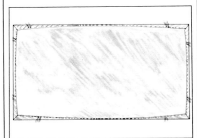

3 Stitch casing/hem in place with an opening on either side of corner.

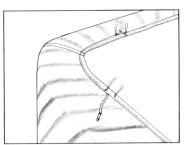

4 Stitch elastic firmly in place, then close both openings.

again (*fig 1*). Fold this marked corner dart with wrong sides facing, matching corner points together; pin and tack. Stitch, 1 cm outside marked line, graduating the stitching down to inner mark. Trim off fabric to within 5 mm of stitching (*fig 2*). Refold dart and stitch again 1 cm from folded edge, forming a French seam.

● Turn under a double 1.5 cm casing/hem all round the outer edge of sheet. Pin. Measure along casing for 34 cm on either side of each corner dart and mark. Tack and stitch round casing, leaving an opening of 1.5 cm at each marked point (*fig 3*).

● Cut four 23 cm-lengths of elastic. Pin first end of one length at one 1.5 cm opening (*fig 4*). Thread opposite end round corner inside casing and pin in opening.

● Pin and stitch across casing just before each opening with two rows of stitching to hold elastic firmly in place. Repeat at each corner. Stitch across each opening to close.

Plain pillowcases

The standard pillow size is 75 cm long by 50 cm wide. To make the pillowcase, use a single piece of extra-wide sheeting fabric.

● Double the length measurement, plus 21 cm for the flap and seam allowance. For the width add 3 cm to width measurement for seam allowance.

● From fabric, cut out one piece to the required size.

● On one short edge, turn a double 5 mm-wide hem to the wrong side; pin, tack and stitch in place. On the opposite short edge, turn 5 cm to the wrong side, turn under raw edge for 1 cm. Pin, tack and stitch across hem, close to inner fold edge.

● Place the fabric flat with wrong side uppermost. Fold in edge with 5 mm-hem to make a 15 cm-deep flap. Press and pin in place. Fold case in half widthways with wrong sides together, so the short edge with wide hem is level with flap edge. Pin, tack and stitch side edges, taking 5 mm seam allowance (*fig 1*).

● Turn pillowcase so right sides are together, with seams to edges. Pin, tack and stitch down sides again, 1 cm from the seamed edge (*fig 2*).

● Turn pillowcase to the right side.

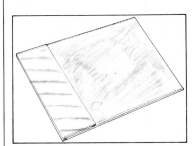

1 Turn in the flap, match front hem to fold edge and stitch sides.

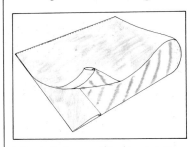

2 Refold with right sides together and complete the French seams.

Frilled pillowcases

Here the canopy fabric is echoed in the bed cushions with a neat double frill in a plain colour taken from the patterned fabric. The plain and lace pillows decorated with toning frills and ribbons complete the picture.

The frill may be single or double, and in a matching or contrasting fabric.

• From the fabric, cut out one back piece to the required size plus 6.5 cm on length and 3 cm on width for seam and hem allowance. Cut out one front adding 3 cm seam allowance to both measurements. Cut out one flap piece the same width as the front and back and 15 cm deep plus 2.5 cm seam allowance.

• For a double frill, allow for twice the length of the complete outer edge. The depth of the frill can be anywhere between 2 cm and 8 cm. Double this width and add 3 cm seam allowance.

• On one short edge of back piece, turn under 5 cm, then tuck under the raw edge for 1 cm. Pin, tack and stitch across hem.

• On one long edge of flap, turn under a double 5 mm hem. Pin, tack and stitch hem in place.

• Cut out sufficient fabric widths for frill. Pin, tack and stitch frill pieces with right sides together into a ring with plain flat seams.

• Fold frill in half lengthways with wrong sides together to form a double frill and pin. Divide the frill into four equal sections and mark. Work two rows of gathering stitches in each frill section in turn (fig 1).

• Divide the outer edge of the front piece into four equal sections and mark (fig 2). Position the frill to right side of front pillowcase, with frill facing in towards the centre. Pull up gathering stitches in each section in turn to match sections on pillowcase. Pin, tack and stitch frill in place.

• With right sides facing, place back on top of frilled front, with hemmed edge adjoining seamline of frill on one short edge. Pin and tack in place (fig 3). Place flap right side down over back hemmed edge of pillowcase, matching long raw edge to short raw edge of front. Pin, tack and stitch all round the pillowcase following the previous stitching. Trim and neaten.

• Turn to right side with the flap on the inside.

Pillowcases with integral borders

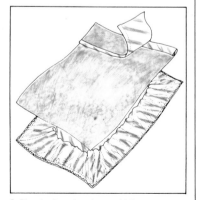

As the border is turned back from the front, only one fabric may be used for this pillowcase.

• From the fabric, cut out the back to the finished size plus 6.5 cm on the length and 3 cm on the width for hem and seam allowance. The flap is 15 cm wide by the finished size plus

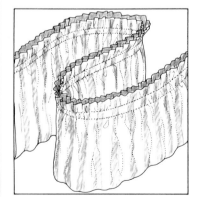

1 Gather up each section of frill with two rows of gathering stitches.

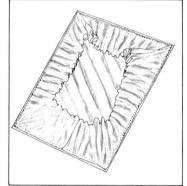

2 Pull up gathering stitches in each section to match up with front piece.

3 Place back against front, add flap on top and stitch together all round.

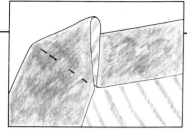

1 Pin out an equal amount of excess fabric at each corner.

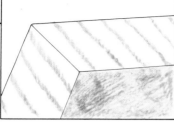

2 Turn under the seam allowance all round the border section.

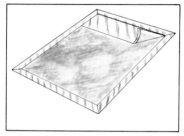

3 Stitch across short edge of pillowcase catching in long raw edge of flap.

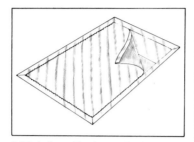

4 Stitch all round border, catching in raw edges of back and flap.

2.5 cm seam allowance on the width and 3 cm seam allowance on the depth. The front is the finished size plus twice the border width all round plus 1.5 cm seam allowance all round. Make the border between 3 cm and 8 cm wide.

● Hem one short edge of back and one long edge of flap as for frilled pillowcase.

● On front, turn border plus 1.5 cm seam allowance to the wrong side. At each corner, pin out excess fabric into a dart, making sure that each corner is the same. Trim off fabric beyond the pinned line. Refold corners with right sides together. Pin, tack and stitch each dart to within 1.5 cm of inner edge (fig 1).

● Turn border to the right side. Press under 1.5 cm along all edges of front border (fig 2).

● Place flap with wrong side to wrong side of front, tucking 1.5 cm on long raw edge and both short edges under front border. Pin, tack

and stitch close to fold along border that contains the flap, stitching from corner to corner (fig 3).

● Place back with wrong side down over flap with hemmed edge against stitched border edge. Tuck all remaining edges under front border. Pin, tack and stitch all round (fig 4).

● Complete by stitching another row of stitching 5 mm from the first row inside the border.

Border pillowcases

As with the frilled design, two contrasting fabrics may be used.

● From fabric cut out back, front and flap pieces as for frilled pillowcase.

● The border should be between 3 cm and 8 cm wide. Double this measurement and add 3 cm seam allowance. For the length, measure one short and one long edge and add twice the width plus 3 cm seam allowance to each measurement. Cut out four border strips to size.

● As for frilled pillowcase, neaten one short edge of flap piece and make a hem on one edge of back.

● Fold each border strip in half lengthways with wrong sides together (fig 1). At each end fold the raw edges to the fold edge at right angles and press. Unfold and cut along pressed line.

● Place border pieces in order: long edge to short edge to long to remaining short edge.

● Open out and place the pieces with right sides together, matching short pointed edges. Pin, tack and stitch to within 1.5 cm of each edge (fig 2). Turn to right side and at the same time refold border in half.

● Position border on right side of front pillowcase; it will split at each corner to form neat turns. Pin, tack and stitch in place (fig 3).

● Place back over front with right sides together, with back hem edge adjoining the seamline and the remaining edges matching. Pin and tack in place.

● Place right side of flap over hemmed edge of back pillowcase, matching long raw edge of flap to short raw edge of front, and remaining raw edges matching raw edges of front and back. Pin, tack and stitch, following previous stitching (fig 4).

● To neaten and strengthen, stitch around pillowcase again 1 cm from previous stitching. Trim and neaten.

● Turn pillowcase to the right side with flap on the inside.

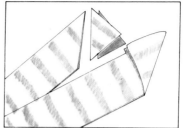

1 Fold each border strip and trim off to form diagonal seam.

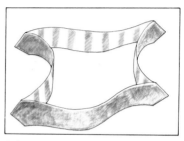

2 Stitch border strips together in the correct order.

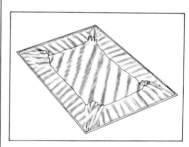

3 Place border against pillowcase front, splitting seams apart at each corner.

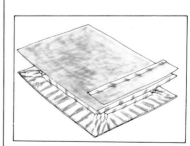

4 Lay back on top of front. Add the flap and stitch all layers together.

▶ Mix plain and patterned fabrics together for a total look in modern bedroom. Fabrics of similar hues work well together for pillowcases, sheets and duvet cover.

Duvets

Duvets come in two basic sizes: double (200 cm × 200 cm) and single (140 cm × 200 cm).

● Cut out two pieces of sheeting fabric to the required size, plus 4 cm seam allowance all round. If the fabric is too narrow, it will be necessary to seam two pieces of fabric together to gain the correct width. Seam together with a plain flat double-stitched seam to give a strong join.

● On the wrong side of each piece, mark in a 2 cm-wide margin all round. Divide the width between the margins into equal sections; on a single duvet make five 28 cm-wide sections, on a double, eight 25 cm-wide sections.

● Cut off a length of tape (5 cm wide, white cotton) for each marked line, the length of the fabric.

● Position the first length of tape at first marked line, overlapping the line by 5 mm; pin in place. Tack and stitch tape in place along marked line, 5 mm from edge of tape (*fig 1*).

● Repeat with remaining lengths of tape along each marked line. Place the two fabric pieces with right sides together matching side edges. Pin, tack and stitch along margin line.

● Refold the fabrics with wrong sides together.

● Working away from the stitched side seam, join the free edge of the first tape to the free fabric piece, again overlapping the marked line by 5 mm. Repeat to stitch each free edge of tape to the free fabric (*fig 2*).

● At the open side, fold both fabric pieces together into a double 1 cm hem. Pin, tack and stitch along hem twice, first close to fold and again about 6 mm away. Close the base edges of the duvet in the same way.

● On the stitched side seam, work two rows of topstitching to match the hemmed side edge (*fig 3*). Peg the top edges of the duvet on to the

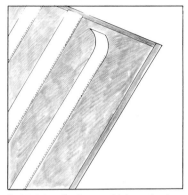

1 Stitch lengths of tape to fabric overlapping marked lines.

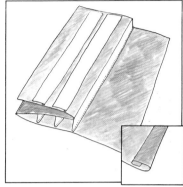

2 Stitch free long edges of tape to second fabric to form channels.

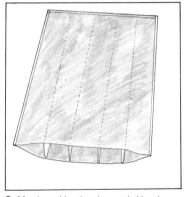

3 Match up side edges by topstitching the seamed edge to match.

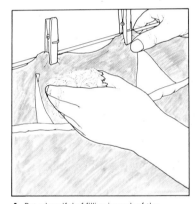

4 Put a handful of filling in each of the channels in turn.

clothes line with the channels open.
● When using a natural filling, put a handful of filling in each channel in turn, closing the channel after each handful (*fig 4*). Repeat until all the filling has been used.
● On synthetic duvets, divide the filling into equal portions for each channel. Fill each channel in turn, pinning it closed afterwards (*fig 5*).
● In both cases, fold the open edges together to form a double 1 cm-wide hem. Then work two rows of stitching across the hem to match the previous edges.

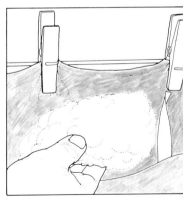

5 After filling the channels, pin together to close, ready for stitching.

Basic duvet covers

As well as extra-wide sheeting, you will need a length of press fastening tape. Alternative fastenings are: touch and close spots, press fasteners or ribbon ties.
● From the fabric, cut out two pieces to the required size, plus 6.5 cm on the length measurement for opening hem and seam allowance, and 3 cm on the width measurement for seam allowance.
● Fold a double 2.5 cm-wide hem along base edge of both cover pieces (*fig 1*). Pin, tack and stitch hems.
● Place cover pieces with right sides together, matching hem edges. Pin, tack and stitch together alongside hem for 30 cm in from each side edge, leaving a central opening.
● Position a length of fastening tape to one half of hem opening. Pin, tack and stitch in place (*fig 2*). Stitch opposite half of tape to opposite hem edge, making sure the fasteners match.
● Fold cover with right sides together. Pin, tack and stitch vertically across the hem edge at each side of opening, enclosing raw edges of fastener tape. Work two rows of stitching for strength (*fig 3*).
● Fold cover with wrong sides together; pin, tack and stitch side edges with French seams. Repeat to stitch top raw edges together with a French seam.
● Turn cover to the right side.

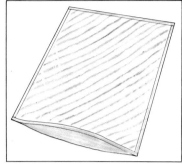

1 Turn a 2.5 cm double hem along base edges of both cover pieces.

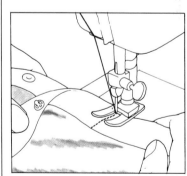

2 Stitch fastening tape into hem opening using a zipper foot on the sewing machine.

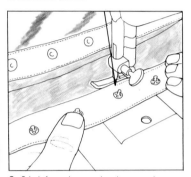

3 Stitch across end of opening to enclose raw edges of tape.

● A frill may be added to the duvet cover. Follow the instructions for frilled pillowcases (page 126), adjusting the measurements to suit your requirements.

Box-pleated valances

For the part of the valance that goes under the mattress, an inexpensive lining fabric can be used.

• Measure the bed base top both ways and cut out one piece to this size adding 4.5 cm to the length and 3 cm to the width for seam and hem allowance. For the pleated flounce, measure the length from bed top to within 1 cm of the floor, adding 6.5 cm allowance. For the width, work out the number and size of the pleats that can be fitted into the bed length and width, making any odd size pleats on either side of the bed top. Arrange for the pleats to meet at the bottom corners. Add on 3 cm allowance at each end.

• Turn under a double 1.5 cm wide hem along top edge of main panel; pin, tack and stitch in place. Pin, tack and stitch flounce widths together into one long length with narrow French seams. Turn under a double 1.5 cm wide hem along both raw side edges of flounce. Pin, tack and stitch in place. At base edge, turn under a double 2.5 cm-wide hem. Pin, tack and stitch hem in place.

• Fold flounce in half widthways and mark centre. Working from the centre, mark out the box pleats. Fold up pleats and pin and tack along the top and base edges (figs 1 + 2).

• Place flounce against three raw

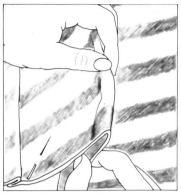

1 Fold up box pleats working from the centre of the base edge of the bed.

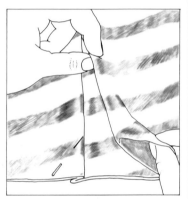

2 After folding up the complete flounce, pin, tack top and base edges to hold.

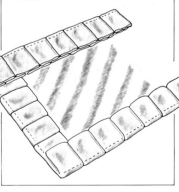

3 Stitch flounce to the three free edges of top, matching hems at top edge.

edges of bed top, matching hem edges at top. Pin, tack and stitch flounce in place (fig 3). Stitch again, then zigzag stitch over raw edges.

Divan covers

These tightly-fitting covers fit all sides of the divan.

• From the fabric cut out one mattress top to the required size, adding 3 cm allowance to both length and width measurements. Cut out each side piece adding seam allowance.

• For flounce, measure length from mattress base to within 1 cm of floor,

adding 6.5 cm for hem and seams. For width, measure each side in turn, adding 23 cm seam allowance. For corner pleats, cut four pieces the same length as the flounce and 23 cm wide.

• Place the side pieces together into a ring in the correct order: long, short, long and remaining short piece. Pin, tack and stitch together, beginning and ending stitching 1.5 cm from seam ends.

• Cut out and make up two lengths of covered piping to fit both sides of the side piece. Position one length of covered piping round top piece, facing inwards and snipping into covering fabric to curve round each corner (fig 1).

• Place side piece and top piece right sides together, splitting seams open at corners. Pin, tack and stitch (fig 2).

• Pin, tack and stitch second length

of covered piping around base edge of side piece in the same way as the first length (*fig 3*).

• Turn a double 2.5 cm-wide hem along base edge of each flounce piece. Pin, tack and stitch hems in place.

• Place flounce pieces in correct order with a pleat section between each piece, with wrong sides together matching hem edges (*fig 4*). Pin, tack and stitch, taking 5 mm seam allowance. Refold each seam with right sides together; pin, tack and stitch; taking 1 cm seam allowance.

• Place flounce against base edge of side piece with right sides together. At each corner fold back the main fabric for 10 cm on each side so the folds meet together at the corner point, forming an inverted pleat with pleat section behind. Pin, tack and stitch together.

◀ A valance can often play a vital role in the overall room design. Here it not only matches the bedlinen, the wallpaper and the wall decoration, it makes the vital aesthetic link between the patterned prints of the walls, pillows and duvet cover, and the plain expanse of the carpet.

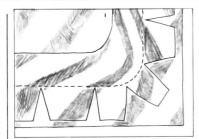

1 Snip into covering fabric to allow piping cord to curve round corner.

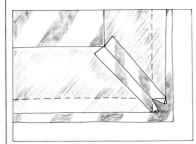

2 The seam will split to help to stitch a right-angle corner.

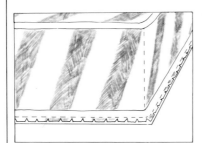

3 Stitch the second length of covered piping round base of side piece.

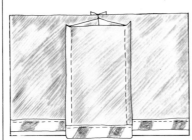

4 Make a box pleat at each corner of the cover.

▲ A fabric valance can soften the line of the bed and disguise its ungainly legs and base. Here the darkest border section of the patterned fabric has been picked out for the valance, and the rest of the bed linen matched in.

Throwover bedspreads

An unlined throwover bedspread is the easiest type to make and the most economical in fabric. A lining does, however, make a neater back to the bedspread and, if lined in quilted fabric, provides an extra layer of warmth. If using a patterned fabric, for a co-ordinated look, line your bedspread in one of the colours picked from the pattern.

● To gauge the size of the bedspread, measure widthways to the floor on either side; repeat lengthways up to the bedhead, allowing for pillow. Add 5 cm all round for the hems.

● To gain the bedspread width, it will be necessary to seam two fabric widths together. To avoid an unsightly centre seam, from fabric cut out two fabric widths to the required length. Fold one fabric piece in half lengthways, matching selvedges together. Carefully cut out along the fold.

If using patterned fabric, ladder-stitch the two half widths to either side of central fabric width. Stitch together with plain, flat seams.

● Press seams open. Trim down the width if necessary to the correct size (plus 5cm hem allowance). Turn under a single 5cm-wide hem on all edges of the bedspread and then press.

● Mitre the corners as follows: unfold pressed hem. Fold in corner across corner point and press (*fig 1*). Refold hem; pin and tack in place. Slipstitch fabric together across corners (*fig 2*).

● Herringbone stitch the hem in place all round the bedspread. Cut out lining to match.

● Place lining against bedspread with wrong sides together, matching seams. Lockstitch the lining to the fabric along the seam allowances (*fig 3*).

● Trim the outer edge of lining level with finished edge all round the bedspread. Turn under a 3 cm single hem on all edges of the lining, mitring the corners in the same way as the fabric.

● Pin, tack and slipstitch the lining to the fabric all round the bedspread (*fig 4*).

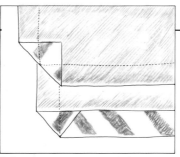
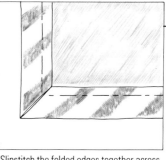

1 Press in corner across point. Refold hems to form a neat mitre.

2 Slipstitch the folded edges together across each corner.

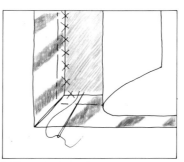
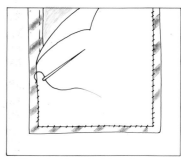

3 After herring-bone stitching the hems, place the lining to the bedspread.

4 Slipstitch with small stitches all round the outer edge of the bedspread.

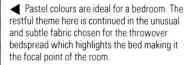 Pastel colours are ideal for a bedroom. The restful theme here is continued in the unusual and subtle fabric chosen for the throwover bedspread which highlights the bed making it the focal point of the room.

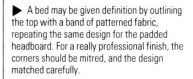 A bed may be given definition by outlining the top with a band of patterned fabric, repeating the same design for the padded headboard. For a really professional finish, the corners should be mitred, and the design matched carefully.

Gathered fitted bedspreads

Gathered fitted bedspreads may be lined or unlined.

• From the fabric cut out one piece for bedspread top to the required size plus 15 cm to 20 cm tuck-over allowance on the length and 3 cm on the width for seam allowances.

• For the length of the gathered flounce, measure from the bed top to within 1 cm of the floor, adding 3 cm for seam allowance. For flounce width, add twice the bed top length to bed top width measurement and double it. Cut out sufficient fabric widths to make up to this length.

• On a double bed the bed top will have to be made up from two fabric widths. Divide one width in half and stitch to either side of remaining fabric width with plain flat seams, matching any pattern across each seam line. (This is to avoid an unsightly centre seam.) Then trim fabric down to correct size.

• Round off the base corners of bed top: position a plate in the corner with edges touching both side and base edges (fig 1). Mark round, then cut round marked line. Fold in half lengthways and mark opposite corner to match. Trim off, as before.

• Divide the bed top from the flounce with covered piping cord. Make up the covered piping cord by

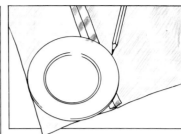

1 Place a plate with edge touching side and base edges. Mark round it.

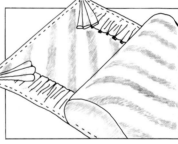

2 After pulling up the gathers in each section, stitch flounce to bed top.

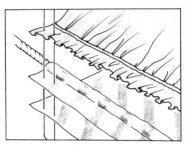

3 Stitch lining bed top to fabric top, across the top edge.

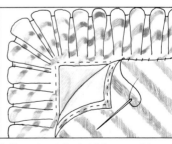

4 Pin, tack and slipstitch lining top to lining flounce.

measuring the length of both side and base edges and making up sufficient length of 5 cm-wide bias fabric strip to cover piping cord. Place piping cord to wrong side of bias strip, fold strip in half evenly round cord; pin, tack and stitch down length. Position covered piping around sides and base edge of bed top, facing inwards. Snip into covering fabric at corners so that the piping will curve around the edge.

• Pin, tack and stitch flounce pieces together with plain, flat seams.

• Cut out and make up the lining flounce in the same way.

• Place fabric and lining flounces with right sides together. Pin, tack and stitch together down side and along base edges. Trim and turn to the right side. Pin and tack top raw edges together.

• Divide the flounce into six equal sections and mark. Divide side and base edges of bed top into six equal sections and mark. Work two rows of gathering stitches along each section of the flounce in turn.

• Position flounce to bed top with right sides together and neatened side edges 1.5 cm down from raw edge of bed top. Pull up gathering stitches in each section in turn to fit each section of the bed top. Pin, tack and stitch flounce to bed top (fig 2).

• Cut out and make up bed top lining as for fabric bed top.

• Position lining top against fabric top with right sides together; pin, tack and stitch in place across top edge (fig 3). Trim and turn lining down over wrong side.

• Turn under side and base edges and pin to flounce, covering previous stitching line and raw edges of allowance. Pin, tack and slipstitch lining top to lining flounce (fig 4).

Canopies

Curtaining above and around the bed adds a touch of glamour and romance and you do not need a four-poster bed to achieve this look.

If you have a four-poster bed the top canopy (or 'roof') can easily be made with a gathered valance to which curtains that meet together at the bottom corners of the bed are added, plus a pair at each side of the bed top. The canopy over the bed can be gathered before the valance frill is added and held in place with touch and close fastenings.

If you do not have a four-poster bed you can give the impression of one with the clever use of draped fabric. The curtains can be hung from a ceiling mounted track, from a coronet or from a curtain pole fixed centrally above the bedhead and held back with tie-backs.

Coronet canopies hang from a semi-circular bracket (or 'coronet') fixed to the wall about 120 cm above the bedhead and covered with fabric, onto which a back and two front curtains are mounted and caught at each side with tie-backs. A simpler method is to hang the drapes from a pole fixed to a curtain pole holder screwed to a ceiling joist.

or to a bracket fixed to the wall above the bedhead. The drapes are then caught at each side with tie-backs.

When choosing a suitable fabric, bear in mind the drape qualities – sheer fabrics can be effective, but need more body to drape successfully over the top of a four-poster bed. Most furnishing cottons will work well, and can be mixed and matched together – for instance, you may choose a plain fabric to hang at the back of the coronet drape behind the bed and a print fabric for the side curtains, adding plain tie-backs. Frills can be added for lavish effect.

▶ A veil of mystery can be brought to the bedroom with a bed canopy in a semi-sheer fabric. Hung on a knotted cord over a ceiling hook, the fabric is caught to a simple lampshade ring, then draped over the corners of the bed.

◀ A properly canopied four-poster bed can take you on a night-time voyage back to the world of Henry VII. Here the rich print gives the impression of Tudor embroidered hangings. The heavy dark carved wood furniture and the sparsely rugged bare wood floor reinforce the late medieval effect.

▲ A length of fabric draped over a short curtain pole provides a simple canopy for a bed. The fabric can be held at the top with a casing and a fabric rosette added to cover the end of the pole.

Simple curtain canopies

These canopies have a central casing which slides over a pole fixed centrally into the wall above the bed (*fig 1*). They are held back by tie-backs at either side of the bed.

● Fix a 4 cm-diameter pole about 45 cm long at the desired height with a 10 cm long dual-ended screw. Alternatively, a decorative pole can be fixed into the ceiling with a decorative bracket at each end. In this case the canopy slots over the pole in between the two brackets.

● Measure from the pole to the floor on one side of the bed, and cut out two pieces to this length by one fabric width. By adding a frill to the front and base edges, you will add to the length and at the same time provide a draped effect.

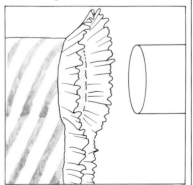

1 Push the canopy over a pole suspended above the bed.

● Pin, tack and stitch the two fabric pieces with right sides together with a plain flat seam. Turn a double 1 cm wide hem along back edges of canopy. Pin, tack and slipstitch hem by hand.

● Make up a double frill for the front and base edges. Cut out 12 cm-wide strips from across the fabric width. When joined together, these will be twice the length of the front and base edges.

● Pin, tack and stitch frill pieces together into one length. Fold frill in half with right sides together. Pin, tack and stitch short edges, from fold to raw edges. Refold frill, with wrong sides together.

● Divide front and base edges of canopy into six equal sections and mark. Divide raw edges of frill into six equal sections and mark. Work two rows of gathering stitches in each of the frill sections in turn.

● Place frill against canopy, right sides together, with seamline of frill 3 cm from raw edge of canopy. Match up each section, pulling up gathers evenly to fit. Pin, tack and stitch frill in place. Trim down seam allowance of frill. Fold seam allowance of fabric in half over raw edges of frill and slipstitch to previous stitches to neaten.

● To form a casing for the pole, fold the canopy in half with wrong sides together and seam at the top Pin, tack and stitch across canopy 6.5 cm from seam, continuing to stitch along frill seamline up to fold, closing the end of the casing.

● If the canopy is to be fixed on brackets in the ceiling, leave both ends of the casing open.

● Make up tie-backs (see page 80)for each side of the canopy and fix to the wall on each side of the bed.

Coronet canopies

These canopies hang from a special coronet or semi-circular bracket fixed to the wall about 130cm above the bedhead. To make the coronet, cut a semi-circle of 25 mm chipboard, 400 mm across the straight back and 250 mm from front to back in the centre. With two angle irons, temporarily fix in place centrally to the wall at the desired height above the bed.

- Measure for the side curtains from the centre of the coronet to the floor in a gentle curve, allowing for the chosen heading tape and hem (a frill can be added to front and base edges of these curtains, if preferred). Measure for the back curtain in the same way, again allowing for the heading tape.
- Unfix the wood to cover both sides with fabric. Cut a piece of fabric the same size as the wood, adding 5 cm all round. Stick to the underside of the wood, bringing the raw edges up and over the outer edges to the top side, snipping into the fabric if necessary to gain a smooth finish.
- Cut another piece of fabric the same size as the top, adding 1 cm all round. Turn under raw edges for 1 cm and stick to the top side, covering previous raw edges (fig 1).
- Fix screw eyes to the underside of the wood 5 mm in from the outer edge, placing them 5 cm apart (fig 2). Make up the back curtain, following instructions for an unlined curtain (see page 70).
- Place curtain hooks through the heading tape and slot these through the screw eyes.
- Make up each side curtain, as an unlined or lined curtain, adding a frill (if desired) and hang as for back curtain so they meet at the centre front of the wood.
- Make tie-backs and fix to the wall on either side of the bed.
- To cover the outer curved edge of the coronet, make up a pleated valance in matching fabric to the required length. Carefully tack in place round the outer curved edge, placing the tacks inside the valance pleats so they are obscured.

An alternative method is to hang the curtains from a track fixed round the outer edge of the wood, with the valance on top to hide the track.

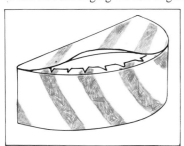

1 Stick the fabric over the top of the coronet covering raw edges.

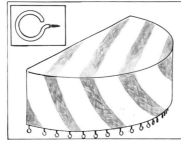

2 Fix screw eyes in place all round outer edge of coronet.

▲ Here brass fitments combine effectively with shimmery semi-transparent fabrics over an ornate four-poster bed. The fabric is caught up into a coronet high over the bed, and then draped round each post with metallic cords and tassels. A traditional lace frill attached to a plain yellow cover adds to the effect.

◀ The effect of the tented ceiling is similar to a canopied look. This bedroom gives total commitment to one patterned fabric. The same design is used for the ceiling, to cover the walls and outline the windows, curtains and bedcover. Large, plain bows at either end of the bolster draw attention to the bedhead.

▲ Fabric held at the bedhead provides a backdrop of material which can be caught up again with a cased pole at the foot of the bed, before knotting up and draping into folds on the floor.

Canopies for four-poster beds

The romantic 'roof' over a four-poster bed is made along the same lines as a 'bagged out' curtain (see page 73).

- Measure between the horizontal poles both ways, adding 3 cm to both measurements for seam allowance. Cut two pieces of fabric to this size for the canopy. For a double bed, two pieces of fabric might have to be joined to achieve the required width. In this case, pin, tack and stitch together with plain flat seams.

- Cut a frill to the required depth, twice the length of each side. Turn and stitch a double 1.5 cm hem along the base edges of each frill piece.

- Work two rows of gathering stitches along the top edge of each frill piece. Place each frill piece against the canopy in turn, right sides and raw edges together, pulling up gathers evenly to fit. Pin and tack in place (*fig 1*).

- Place second canopy piece on top of first, right sides together. Pin, tack and stitch together all round, catching in frill, and leaving a central opening in one long side. Trim and turn to the right side. Turn in open-

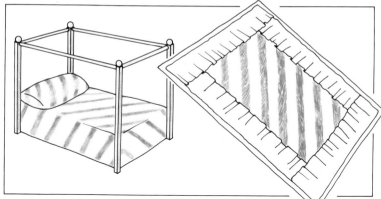

1 Pin and tack frill pieces to each side of the canopy in turn.

◄ A four-poster bed effect can be achieved by fitting a simple track to the ceiling from which the curtains are hung. Finish with a simple heading tape and allow for one curtain on either side of base corners and one on each side of the bedhead. Matching the fabrics throughout makes for a totally restful bedroom.

ing edges in line with the remainder of the seam and slipstitch to close.

• Place the canopy so that the frill sections hang over the horizontal poles. If the fabric has a tendency to slip, stitch touch and close discs along the seamlines and stick the opposite halves to the poles to correspond.

• If you want to gather up the centre canopy, cut out the main pieces one-and-a-half times the required length. Work two rows of gathering stitches along both side edges and pull up to the correct size. Stitch down both sides to hold gathers in place. Then add the frill sections as before.

• Curtains can be added to a four-poster bed, either lined or unlined. Make up six curtains (see page 70), two for each long side and one for each end, so that when drawn back, there will be a curtain on either side of the bedhead and one on either side of the two end posts. Hold back the curtains with tie-backs fixed to the wall at the bedhead or to the end posts.

• As an alternative, when you do not have the framework of a four-poster, fix a ceiling-mounted curtain track the same size and shape as the bed (mitre the track at the corners) in place above the bed. Make up curtains, tying them together as described.

▶ Lined with semi-sheer fabric, these four-poster curtains are made in the same pattern fabric as the bedcover. As with windows, lined curtains dramatically reduce head loss and in this case provide insulation with the timeless grace of the four-poster. Here the two side curtains are caught-up with tie-backs, leaving the base free. The valanced top is outlined with a heavy fringe in toning colours which emphasise the shaped edge.

Accessories

It's not enough just to get the big things right. To create a complete atmosphere every little detail – the table napkins, the lampshades and the basket linings – should match too. Fortunately, it is quick and easy to furnish these finishing touches.

▶ Total co-ordination is achieved here by matching up the curtains and seat covers to the tablecloth and lampshade. You may choose, as here, to make the statement with beautifully matched fabrics, keeping the styles plain and uncluttered.

Round tablecloths

Round tables look particularly pretty with lacy square cloths placed on top of full-length circular ones.

● To find the size of a full-length cloth, measure the diameter of the table top, then the distance from the top edge of the table to the floor. Double this measurement and add it to the table-top diameter. Add 1.5 cm all round for the hem.

● To make a pattern for one quarter of the cloth, cut a piece of brown paper slightly larger than a quarter of the desired size of the tablecloth.

● Cut a length of string 20 cm longer than quarter of the diameter. Take a pencil and notch into the end nearest the point. Tie one end of the string round this notched end. Fasten a drawing pin through the centre of the string and corner point with the string exactly the length of

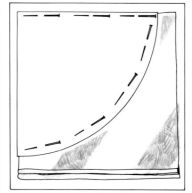

1 Match centre points when pinning the paper pattern to the fabric.

the quarter-diameter measurement. Draw an arc with the string taut across the paper from one side to the other. Remove string and pin. Carefully cut along marked line.

If the cloth is large the fabric will have to be seamed to gain the required width. Follow instructions for rectangular tablecloths or use a wide-width fabric.

● Fold fabric in half lengthways then in half widthways, matching outer edges and seamlines. Pin outer edges together. Pin paper pattern to fabric, matching centre points (*fig 1*). Carefully cut out round outer edge. Remove pattern and unfold fabric.

● Stitch all round the outer edge of the cloth, 1.5 cm from the edge. This stitching line marks the finished edge of the cloth. Press in the outer edge along stitching line to the wrong side of the fabric.

● Turn in the raw edge inside the hem, so the hem is halved. Keep measuring as the hem is pinned, to check that it remains the same width all round the edge. Pin, tack and stitch hem in place.

Rectangular tablecloths

Apart from its practical function, a tablecloth can enhance the décor, especially if you choose a fabric to match the curtains, for instance.

Provençal-printed fabrics bring that summery feel to the breakfast table. Padded tablemats have matched mitred corners while the border sections are quilted with parallel rows of stitching. Keep the napkins plain, in a bright print fabric of the same hues as the mats.

▶ Cone-shaped lampshades are easy to make in a fabric that matches the room's décor. Both Top and base can be edged with a simple braid to add definition.

● Measure the table top and decide how far you want your cloth to hang down the sides, adding 3 cm hem allowance. If the total measurement is wider than the fabric, cut out one central panel and then one piece the same length and cut in half lengthways. Pin, tack and stitch each half width to either side of central panel with flat fell seams. This is simply to avoid an unsightly seam down the centre of the tablecloth.

● Press 1.5 cm to the wrong side along each edge of the fabric. Fold over and press a further 1.5 cm.

● To mitre the corners, open out the last hem fold. Cut across the corner to within 6 mm of the corner point. Fold back the corner with right sides together, matching cut edges.

● Pin and stitch across the corner, stitching through the corner point. Press seam flat. Turn corner through

to the right side, refolding the double hem. Pin, tack and stitch all round the hem. Alternatively, bind the raw edges with bias binding in a contrasting colour.

Napkins

Napkins are usually between 45 cm and 50 cm square so that two can be cut from across the fabric width. Four tea-time napkins measuring about 20 cm square can be cut out from across the fabric width.

The design of your napkin does not have to be this strict though. You can make them almost any size and shape and out of any thick, relatively absorbent material.
- On each napkin, turn a double 7 mm hem on all edges, folding neat corners.
- Pin, tack and stitch all round the napkin hem.

Tablemats

Tablemats are usually rectangular (30 cm by 20 cm) or round (20-25 cm across). Either use quilting fabric or sandwich thin wadding between two layers of fabric, and finish the raw edges with bias binding.
- Cut out two pieces of pre-quilted fabric and one piece of lightweight wadding to the required size. Place fabric with wrong sides together, sandwiching wadding in between. Pin and tack together all round.
- Make up a length of 5 cm-wide bias binding. Fold in both long edges and press. Unfold one edge and place against one side of outer edge of mat. Stitch short edges of binding together to fit.
- Pin, tack and stitch binding in place along crease. Fold binding over raw edges of mat to the opposite side. Pin, tack and stitch in place round the edge of the mat, folding corners into mitres, if necessary.

Bonded card lampshades

To make a bonded card lampshade you will need two lampshade rings, adhesive cotton tape, bonded card for the shade and the fabric of your choice. To make a shaped shade, either a cone or coolie, you will need to make a pattern. (On a drum shade there is no need to make a pattern as the shape is straight.)
- On a sheet of paper, mark a base line AB (the length being the diameter of the bottom lampshade ring) and mark in the centre point.
- Draw a line up from the centre point. Mark off the desired height of the lampshade, C. Mark another horizontal line DE, through point C, to correspond with the length of the diameter of the top ring.
- Mark a line from B through E until it crosses the centre line at F. Repeat on the opposite side from A through D to F.
- Notch the pointed end of a pencil. Knot a length of string round the pencil. Place the point of the pencil on B and fasten a drawing pin through the centre of the string at F with the string stretched taut. Draw an arc through A and B and mark up on either side of these points. Repeat to mark an arc through points DE.
- With the centre line as the centre point of the measurement, mark the circumference of the bottom ring along the bottom arc. Repeat to mark the circumference of the top ring along the top arc. Join up the ends of the lines with F.
- Cut out the pattern formed, adding an overlap of 2cm on one side. Check the pattern by holding it in place on the lampshade rings with clothes pegs.
- Stick adhesive cotton tape around both lampshade rings. Press fabric. Peel off backing from one side of bonding card and carefully press to wrong side of fabric, making sure that there are no air bubbles.
- Mark around lampshade pattern on the wrong side of bonded fabric, with centre line of pattern to straight of grain of fabric. Carefully cut out.
- Hold shade against rings with clothes pegs, marking in overlap on the wrong side. Stick overlap in place. Stick lampshade rings in place.
- If desired, stick braid round top and bottom edges, butting ends together.

Pleated paper lampshades

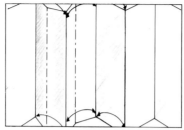

Wallpaper is ideal for pleated lampshades and means you can exactly match your décor, if you wish. Apart from the wallpaper for the shade you will need two lampshade rings and a leather punch.

● Measure the circumference of the base lampshade ring and double the measurement. Cut out a length of wallpaper to this length by the desired height of the shade.

● On the wrong side of the paper, mark lines 4cm apart from top to bottom, making sure that each line is at right angles to the long edges.

● Fold back the paper along each marked line and press in crease. To form the pleats, take the first fold and place it against the next creased line and press well. Continue to end (*fig 1*). (Each pleat 2cm wide.)

● With right side facing, punch a hole in the centre of each pleat, 1.3cm in from long edges.

● Thread a temporary length of cotton through all the holes at both top and bottom; draw up round the lampshade rings and knot to hold.

● Overlap and stick the ends together, making sure that the raw edge is on the inside of a pleat.

● Holding the top ring inside the pleated paper and working with a double thread, begin by knotting the thread to the ring. Lace the pleats to the ring, by pushing the needle

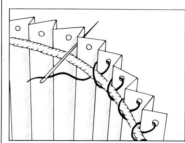

1 Take the first fold and place against the next creased line; press.

2 Loop thread under and over ring and push needle to right side.

through the left-hand hole of the first pleat to the right side.
Then bring needle back to the inside through the hole to the right.

● Loop the thread under and over the lampshade ring and push the needle to the right side through the left-hand hole of the next pleat (*fig 2*). Work back to the inside through the right-hand hole. Repeat to lace all the pleats to the ring, pulling up the thread as you work, so the pleats just rest against the ring. Lace the paper shade to the bottom ring in the same way. Remove thread.

● If you require a trimming, thread a length of decorative ribbon or braid through the loops and tie into a bow. The top and bottom edges can also be fitted with a length of ribbon or braid or with a strip of contrasting wallpaper. Simply stick raw edges together before pleating the paper.

Coat-hanger covers

Satin or pre-quilted cotton are suitable fabrics for covering a wooden coat-hanger.

● If using plain cotton, add an extra layer underneath the outer cover.

● You will need a length of 6mm-wide ribbon to wrap around the hook. Begin at the hook end, tucking in the end of the ribbon to hold. Then bind round the hook diagonally, overlapping slightly each time. At the base of the hook, pull the end of the ribbon through the last layer to knot. (Tuck this end into the cover when it is stitched into position.)

● Bind the hanger with a 5cm-wide strip of medium-weight wadding. Stick the end in place with fabric adhesive, then wind diagonally over the hanger at right angles to the hook. At the opposite end, fasten the wadding in place with small stitches.

● Cut a piece of pre-quilted fabric on the bias of the fabric, 10cm wider and longer than the hanger. Fold fabric in half lengthways; place the hanger inside with base against the fold; pin.

● Trimming as you stitch, turn in 1cm of raw edge at rounded side and top edges of hanger and stitch together with small neat stitches, stitching carefully round the hook. Fasten off at opposite end.

Moses basket linings

To make a lining for a Moses basket, use either pre-quilted fabric or make up your own using a medium-weight wadding, backing fabric and the cotton fabric of your choice. Various trimmings can be added.

● Measure the outside of the base both ways. Mark the centre of the side edges of the basket, then measure from centre point round the basket top to centre point, and the depth at the highest point. Repeat to measure round the base edge of the basket.

● From pre-quilted fabric or from fabric, backing fabric and medium weight wadding, cut out a rectangle of fabric for base and for both side pieces to these measurements, adding 5cm all around.

● If quilting the fabric, place the fabric and backing fabric with wrong sides together, sandwiching the wadding in between. Quilt through the three layers to form small squares or a diamond-shape pattern.

● Place the basket on the wrong side of the base rectangle and mark round the outside of the basket. Mark centre of side edges of base.

● Place side rectangles with right sides together; pin, tack and stitch side seams. Trim and neaten.

● Work two rows gathering stitches round base edge of side piece.

● Matching seams to centres, place

▲ A pleated shade can be made from wallpaper or wrapping paper. Here the effect achieved is of graduations of colour. Combined with a shiny cylindrical base, this makes a modern light fitment to brighten up a corner of the room.

side piece against base with right sides together, pulling up gathers evenly to fit. Pin, tack and stitch together. Trim and neaten seam.

• Place lining inside basket and mark round the top edge on the wrong side of the fabric (fig. 1). Remove lining from basket.

• Bind the raw top edge: unfold one edge of 2.5cm-wide bias binding; place against right side of cover with creased line matching marked line on cover. Pin, tack and stitch in place, stitching raw edges of binding together at one centre seam to fit. Trim fabric and then fold binding over top raw edge; pin, tack and slip-stitch remaining edge of binding in place to previous stitching line on the wrong side of the lining.

• To add a trimming, match the edge of a length of pre-gathered lace, for example, to edge of binding on right side of lining, and stitch raw edges together at one centre seam to fit. Stitch trimming in place.

• To make a tie for each handle, place lining inside basket and mark positions of handles. Cut a 75cm length of bias binding for each tie. Turn in raw ends for 6mm, then fold binding in half lengthways. Pin, tack and stitch all round tie. Position centre of ties at handle positions on wrong side of the cover. Fix in place

with two rows of stitching (fig 2).

• To add a frill to the top of the basket, mark the edge of the lining 3cm above the edge of the basket and then bind as before. Measure top edge of basket and double it.

• Cut out sufficient 20cm wide strips to this length for the frill. Pin, tack and stitch frill pieces together into a ring with flat fell seams.

• Turn a double 6mm hem along bottom edge of frill; pin, tack and stitch. Turn down top edge of frill for 5mm, then for a further 4.5cm. Work two rows of gathering stitches round frill top, 3cm and 3.5cm from top.

• Place lining inside basket. Pin frill to outside edge of cover, pulling up gathers evenly to fit. Remove from basket; pin, tack and stitch frill in place between gathering stitches, beginning and ending at handle positions on either side. At these positions just stitch through frill gathers to hold them in place.

• Stitch trimming round inside of lining, by hand. Cover gathering stitches on outside of lining by hand-stitching ribbon all round frill.

• Place the lining inside the basket and mark positions for press fasteners between frill and lining round handles. Remove from the basket and stitch press fasteners in place. This makes the cover detachable.

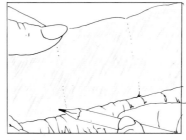

1 Mark round top edge of basket on wrong side of lining.

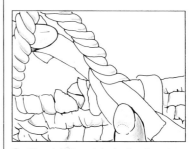

2 Thread tie through basket handle to right side and fasten into a bow.

Hammocks

Only hard-wearing fabrics like canvas are suitable for hammocks, and you will need 24 m of strong 1 cm in diameter rope to form the hanging loops.

- To judge how much fabric you will need, calculate your height, plus 20 cm, plus 60 cm for loops, by 140 cm wide.

- Cut out a length of canvas to required size. Using a ruler and set square, divide each end into eight even sections, each one about 18 cm wide. Draw a line in from each mark for 30 cm at right angles to the side edges of the hammock. Cut along each marked line (fig 1).

- Turn and press 1 cm to the wrong side across the ends of each strip. Stitch in place, fastening off well at each end. Turn and press a double 1 cm wide hem on the long edges of each strip, graduating the hem down round the inner corners. Stitch. Work round each inner corner with a tight zigzag stitch to reinforce the curves (fig 2).

- Turn back 5 cm on each strip and then a further 12 cm to form the hanging loops. Pin and stitch in place with two rows of stitching spaced 5 mm apart. Repeat with two more rows of stitching 5 mm apart, 5 cm up from previous stitching. Fasten off each row of stitching securely.

- Lay the hammock flat. Insert rope through all loops at one end pulling

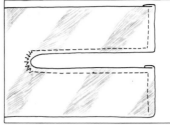

1 Divide up each end and mark in at right-angles to form the loops.

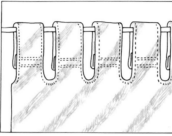

2 Reinforce the hems round the tight corners with zigzag stitching.

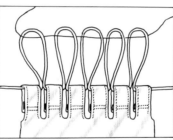

3 Thread the rope through the fabric, leaving rope loops in between.

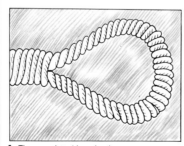

4 The completed hanging loop.

out about 2 m at opposite end (fig 3) and 100 cm-long loops at each gap. Cut off excess rope, leaving 2 m.

Take the excess rope at both sides and fasten back on itself with three to four half-hitch knots.

Tie a piece of string round loops at mid-point. Tie two string markers 10 cm on either side of the central string.

Bind round loops from one marker, through centre, to second marker, tucking in cord end firmly. Bring all ropes together, then continue to bind over the combined ropes for 4 cm to form a strong loop for hanging. Thread in cord securely (fig 4).

Repeat to form a hanging loop at opposite end of hammock.

- Add a decorative braid to sides of hammock if desired.

Directors' chairs

Recovering a folding chair is a simple task as long as the frame is sound. Canvas or heavyweight cotton fabrics are most suitable. To fix, you will need a special fabric stapler or upholstery nails.

- Either remove the old covers and use them as a pattern for the new ones, or measure the open frame to gauge the size of each piece.

- Cut out one piece for the seat, adding 8 cm to the length and 6 cm to the width. Zigzag stitch along front and back edges of seat.

- Turn a 4 cm-single hem along

▶ Folding directors' chairs will have to be protected from the elements. Although you would not expect to leave them out anyway, they are best sited under shelter to protect them from sudden showers. The fabric should be shrink-proof, of course. But you should also make sure that it will not fade in direct sunlight.

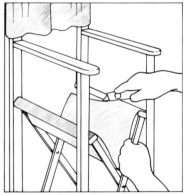

1. Remove the old covers with a Stanley knife if necessary.

back edge of seat to wrong side. Pin and stitch in place with two rows of stitching 5 mm apart. Repeat at front edges. Zigzag stitch both side edges.

- Position seat centrally over frame, turn under zigzagged side edges for about 3 cm and staple to the wooden frame spacing staples about 2 cm apart, with one positioned at each

1 Place canvas against top bar and staple firmly in position.

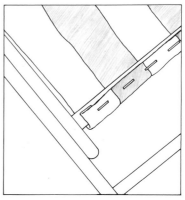

2 Staple round bottom bar, turning under excess canvas at sides if necessary.

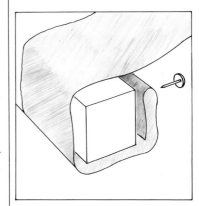

3 Alternatively, fix canvas in place with upholstery nails.

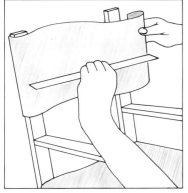

2 Use the old covers as a pattern or measure the open frame.

end (*fig 1*). Open out frame and check that the seat is taut. If saggy, remove one side and re-staple, turning under extra canvas.

● Cut out the back, adding 8 cm to length and 3 cm plus sufficient allowance for casing round side struts to the width. Zigzag stitch and hem front and back edges as for seat.

● Make a 1 cm fold along both of the shorter sides of the cover and a second larger fold to form a casing to fit over the side struts. Machine stitch the casings.

● Slot the canvas back over the wooden uprights of the chair.

Deckchairs

The bottom end of most deckchairs is slightly narrower than the top end, so you may need to fold the corners under to taper the width of the fabric.

● Either remove the old canvas and use it as a pattern for the new canvas,

or measure the deckchair frame by laying the frame flat and measuring twice round the fixing rail at the top and then to bottom of frame.

● Using a set square and a rule, square off the end of the new canvas. Then cut out the correct length.

● Zigzag stitch along the raw edges at both ends of the canvas. Place the top edge of the canvas against the top bar of the chair frame (*fig 1*). Staple in place at each end and with staples spaced about 2 cm apart in between.

● Wind the canvas once round the bar. Turn frame over and pull canvas taut round bottom bar. Staple in place as before (*fig 2*).

● As an alternative, hammer canvas to frame using upholstery nails (*fig 3*). If the canvas is wider than the frame, do not trim but turn under an equal amount at each side before fixing in place.

Glossary

Acorn
A plastic or wooden bead enclosing the pulling cord that act as the lever on roller blinds.

Appliqué
A design compiled of pieces of fabric applied onto the background of another fabric. The fabrics can be sewn, stuck or fused into position.

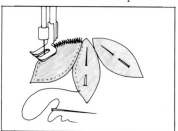

Architrave
Decorative wood edging.

Battening
A thin strip of wood.

Beading
Semi-circular wood moulding used to finish edges in a decorative way.

Bias binding
Strips of material cut on the diagonal grain of the fabric used to bind raw fabric edges or for covering piping cord. Can be bought readymade or can be cut from fabric as follows: fold the selvedge at right angles across the fabric parallel to the weft (see p. 67 for illustration). The bias will run at 45° to the fabric grain. Cut the strips along the bias.

Blanket stitch
Used to neaten raw edges or provide a decorative edge. Work from left to right with the fabric edge facing you. Fasten the working thread with a couple of back stitches, then insert the needle in the fabric and bring out under the fabric edge, over the working thread. Pull through. Reinsert the needle the same distance from the edge, and the required distance from the previous stitch and bring out under the fabric edge and over the working thread, as before. Continue in this way. To finish, secure the last stitch over a loop and fasten off on the wrong side of the fabric.

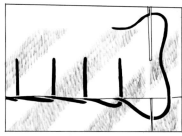

Blind stitching
Used in upholstery to hold the filling in place on a seat, between the central ties and the rolled edge.

Bridle ties
In upholstery, bridle ties form large loops round the centre of the seat to hold the filling in place.

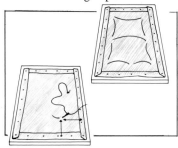

Bump
Fabric made from cotton waste and used as an interlining for curtains.

Casing
A channel formed by a row of stitching a certain distance from a folded or seamed edge or by working two parallel rows of stitching. Used to house elastic, laths, etc.

Castellation
A square evenly-shaped edge, similar to castle battlements.

Cleat
A two-pronged hook positioned at the side of a window round which cords are wound in a figure of eight to secure them.

Dart
Method of disposing of fullness in fabric by matching up two points on the outer edge and graduating the stitching from the matched points into a centre point.

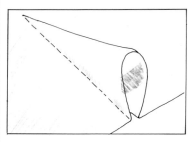

Domette
A cotton/wool mix flannel – cotton warp, woollen weft – used for curtain interlining.

Double hem
A self-neatening hem, where the fabric is turned up twice for the same amount, enclosing the raw edge.

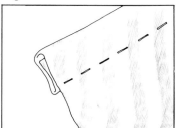

Eyelet
Metal holes, of varying size, that can be fixed to fabric to close an opening. Eyelets can also be worked by hand, by punching a hole and buttonhole stitching around the raw edge.

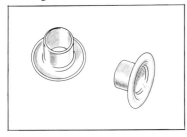

Facing
A piece of fabric stitched to a raw edge to neaten.

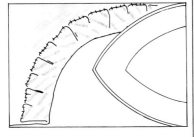

Finial
A decorative end piece on a curtain pole or track.

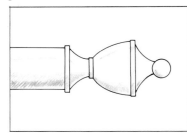

Flat fell seam
The most used self-neatening seam in soft furnishings. Place the two fabrics with right sides together. Pin, tack and stitch together, 1.5 cm from the raw edges. Trim down one seam allowance to 5 mm. Fold the wider seam allowance in half, with raw edge to seamline, enclosing the narrower seam allowance, then press flat against the wrong side of the fabric. Pin, tack and stitch down seam again, close to folded edge.

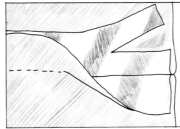

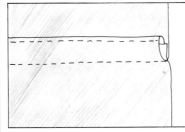

Flounce
A skirt of fabric, which can be plain, gathered or pleated around a valance, bedspread, divan cover, etc.

French seam
A self-neatening seam, used for sheer and fine fabrics. Place the fabrics with wrong sides together. Pin, tack and stitch 5 mm from the raw edges. Trim down both seam allowances to 3 mm. Refold with right sides together and with seam to edge. Pin, tack and stitch down seam again, 1 cm from edge.

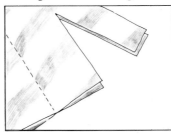

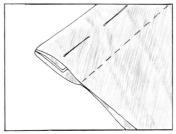

Glider
A small component that runs along curtain track and holds the curtain hooks. Hook/gliders combine the two.

Grain
The direction in which the fibres of fabric or wood run.

Gusset
The side section (eg, of a cushion), positioned between top and bottom sections to give depth.

Half-hitch knot
A knot made by wrapping the rope round itself and then through the loop that is formed, which is then pulled tight.

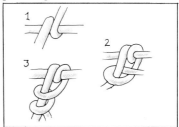

151

Herringbone stitch
Used to fasten single hems in place when making curtains, etc. Secure the working thread under the hem. Bring the thread through the hem 3-5 mm from edge. Working diagonally, take a tiny stitch in the main fabric from right to left. Bring the needle diagonally back down to hem edge and take a small stitch from right to left. Continue to the end, then secure the thread inside the hem.

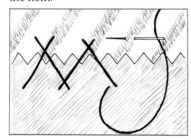

Joist
A wooden beam on the ceiling to which heavy items can be fixed.

Ladderstitch
The professional way to tack two pieces of patterned fabric together and produce the perfect match across a seamline. Press under 1.5 cm seam allowance on first piece of fabric and position 1.5 cm over second fabric piece, matching the pattern exactly. Pin together. Secure the working thread with a knot inside the seam. Then, working from the right side, take the needle into the flat fabric and out again about 1.5 cm along the seamline. Take needle directly across the join and up through the folded edge of second fabric for about 1.5 cm. Continue up the seam in this way, forming 'steps' of thread. The fabric can then be folded with right sides

together and the seam stitched in the usual way.

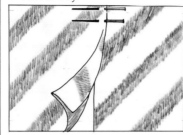

Lath
A thin length of wood that provides weight in the bottom casing of a blind, for instance.

Lockstitch
The professional way to join two layers of fabric loosely together (lining to curtain, for example), allowing for a certain amount of give between the two layers. Position fabric wrong side up; place lining on top, pin together slightly to the left of the centre. Fold back the lining and, using thread that matches the fabric, secure the working thread with a knot on the wrong side of the lining. Take a small stitch through lining and fabric (one thread only), taking needle over the working thread. Continue along the complete length, leaving the thread very loose. Work rows of lockstitching about 30-40 cm apart.

Mitre
The technical term for reducing the bulk when turning a hem (as on curtains) or applying a trimming round a corner. It is the diagonal seamline formed at 45 degrees to the sides.

Motif
The dominant part of a design.

Nap
A soft, raised surface on a fabric produced by a finishing process.

Patchwork
The art of joining small shaped pieces of fabric together to gain a larger piece while producing an attractive design.

Pelmet
A length of stiffened fabric fixed above curtains concealing the track.

Pinking shears
Serrated scissors that are used for neatening edges. Not to be used for cutting out.

Piping
An attractive and professional finish to seamlines on home furnishings such as loose covers and cushions. Piping can be corded or flat and in both cases the covering fabric must be cut on the bias. In corded piping the bias strip is folded evenly in half round a cotton piping cord. This cord can be purchased in various thicknesses and must be pre-shrunk before use. Flat piping consists of the bias strip used folded in half, flat. Once the cord has been enclosed the two types are applied in the same way along the seamline between two fabric pieces. The bias strip can be snipped up to the stitching to help to turn corners. When the piped edges meet round a shape, they can

be joined by trimming down the cord so the ends butt together. Trim the fabric strip so the overlap is 1 cm. Turn under one end for 5 mm and place over opposite raw edge. Stitch across join.

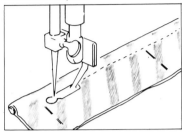

Plain flat seam
The simplest method of stitching two pieces of fabric together. Place fabric pieces with right sides together. Pin, tack and stitch together, taking 1.5 cm. Work a few stitches in reverse at each end of stitching to hold firmly in place. Neaten and press open or to one side.

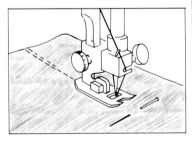

Quilting
The method used to join two layers of fabric with a wadded centre together in a decorative way.

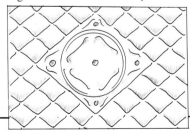

Scallop
A curved edge based on the scallop shell, used as decoration for pelmets, roller blinds, etc. The easiest way to make a scallop pattern is to use a round object such as a plate positioned on squared pattern paper, so that each scallop can be marked out the same size. Divide the edge to be covered to find the best size for the scallop.

Screw eye
A metal screw with a round eyelet head.

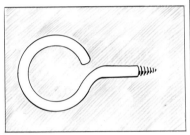

Scrim
An open weave hessian made from flax, used in upholstery to cover the seat filling.

Selvedge
The non-fray tightly-woven edge of fabric that runs down each side parallel with the warp (see p. 67 for illustration).

Sheer
A transparent or semi-transparent fabric used for net curtains.

Single hem
A simple hem, in which the fabric is turned up only once to the wrong side, leaving the raw edge.

Skirting board
A length of wood fastened in place around the base of walls to finish and protect them.

Slipstitch
This stitch is used to join two folded edges together across an opening. Pin and tack the folded edges together. Fasten the working thread inside one folded edge. Bring out the needle from the fold and take a stitch about 3 mm long in the opposite fold. Repeat, working through each fold in turn, to produce tiny invisible stitches across the opening.

Strut
A turned piece of wood that forms the back of a chair.

Swag
A traditional way of arranging loose fabric as a pelmet. The fabric is wound round the curtain pole in large loops or swags and falls into shaped tails at each side of the window.

Slub
A lumpy effect in woven fabric, made by uneven warp thread.

Tack
A small nail with a large flat head and sharp pointed end used in upholstery.

Tacking
A basic stitch used either for tracing out a shape or for holding two or more layers of fabric together ready for permanent stitching. Basic tacking is simply a large running stitch worked in and out of the fabric. Begin with a knot and work a back stitch at the end to hold. Tacking can also be worked unevenly or diagonally.

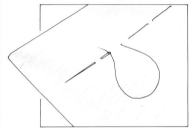

Toggle
An oblong plastic or wooden button with one central hole.

Topstitching
A row of straight stitching worked on the right side of the fabric.

Touch and close spots
Fasteners consisting of two small circles of nylon. One circle is covered with small soft loops and the opposite circle is covered with small firm hooks. When pressed together the two circles interlock.

Valance
A short, soft, frilly edge for curtain tops or bed linen.

Wadding
A padding made from cotton, wool, or synthetic fibres. Usually 90 cm. wide, it comes in three thicknesses and is used in quilting, upholstery, etc.

Warp
Parallel strands of fibres running the length of the fabric, interlacing with weft threads (see p. 67 for illustration).

Webbing
Woven fabric strip usually 5 cm wide used in upholstery. Black and white webbing is the strongest, used for upholstering seats. Beige jute webbing can be used for seat backs.

Weft
Yarn which runs from side to side across the fabric width, interlacing with warp threads (see p. 67 for illustration).

Zigzag stitch
A sewing-machine stitch which can be used to neaten seams functionally or decoratively. The size and density of the stitch can be altered to gain a satin stitch for appliqué for instance – a large spaced stitch to hold down a decorative cord.

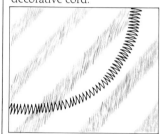

CONVERSION CHART

Metric	Imperial	Metric	Imperial	Metric	Imperial
3mm	$\frac{1}{8}$in	10cm	4in	1m (100cm)	39$\frac{1}{2}$in (3ft 3$\frac{1}{2}$in)
6mm	$\frac{1}{4}$in	20cm	7$\frac{7}{8}$in	2m	79in (6ft 7in)
10mm (1cm)	$\frac{3}{8}$in	25cm	10in	3m	118$\frac{1}{2}$in (9ft 10$\frac{1}{2}$in)
1.5cm	$\frac{5}{8}$in	30cm	11$\frac{3}{4}$in	4m	158in (13ft 2in)
2cm	$\frac{3}{4}$in	35cm	13$\frac{3}{4}$in (1ft 1$\frac{3}{4}$in)	5m	237in (19ft 9in)
2.5cm	1in	40cm	15$\frac{3}{4}$in (1ft 3$\frac{3}{4}$in)	6m	252in (21ft)
3cm	1$\frac{1}{8}$in	45cm	17$\frac{3}{4}$in (1ft 5$\frac{3}{4}$in)	7m	276$\frac{1}{2}$in (23ft 0$\frac{1}{2}$in)
4cm	1$\frac{1}{2}$in	50cm	19$\frac{3}{4}$in (1ft 7$\frac{3}{4}$in)	8m	316in (26ft 4in)
5cm	2in	60cm	23$\frac{1}{2}$in (1ft 11$\frac{1}{2}$in)	9m	355$\frac{1}{2}$in (29ft 7$\frac{1}{2}$in)
6cm	2$\frac{3}{8}$in	70cm	27$\frac{1}{2}$in (2ft 3$\frac{1}{2}$in)	10m	395in (32ft 11in)
7cm	2$\frac{3}{4}$in	75cm	29$\frac{1}{2}$in (2ft 5$\frac{1}{2}$in)	20m	790in (65ft 10in)
8cm	3$\frac{1}{8}$in	80cm	31$\frac{1}{2}$in (2ft 7$\frac{1}{2}$in)	30m	1185in (98ft 8$\frac{1}{2}$in)
9cm	3$\frac{1}{2}$in	90cm	35$\frac{1}{2}$in (2ft 11$\frac{1}{2}$in)	40m	1580in (131ft 8in)
10cm	4in	100cm (1m)	39$\frac{1}{2}$in (3ft 3$\frac{1}{2}$in)	50m	1975in (164ft 7in)

Sources

DUVET FILLINGS

Limericks
117 Victoria Avenue,
Southend-on-Sea, Essex
(also wide-width sheeting and
featherdown proof fabric)

FABRIC

Busby & Busby
57 Salisbury Street, Blandford
Forum,
Dorset DT11 7PY

Designers Guild
271 & 277 Kings Road,
London SW3 5EN

Christian Fischbacher
Threeways House,
42-44 Clipstone Street,
London W1

Habitat
Hithercroft Road,
Wallingford – and branches
throughout the UK

Heal's
196 Tottenham Court Road,
London W1

Interior Selection
240 Blythe Road, London W14

John Lewis
Oxford Street, London W1
(also wide-width sheeting, blind
kits and cushion and bolster pads)

Liberty & Co. Ltd.
Regent Street,
London W1

Machinka
The Mail House, Eldon Street,
Tuxford, Newark, Notts NG22 1DO

Martex & Co
Lonbury House, Green Lane,
London N13

Nice Irma's
46 Goodge Street, London W1

Osborne & Little
304 Kings Road, London SW3 5UH

Paper Moon
12-13 Kingswell, 59-62 Heath Street,
London NW3 1EN

Russell & Chapple
23 Monmouth Street, London WC2
(canvas fabric)

Arthur Sanderson Ltd.
53 Berners Street, London W1

Tissunique Ltd.
10 Princes Street,
Hanover Square,
London W1

Warners
7-11 Noel Street, London W1

For a complete list of fabric outlets
in the UK, contact the West End
Furnishing Fabrics Association at
Stransky Thompson PR, 26 Lloyd
Baker Street, London WC1X 9AU.

FELT AND HESSIAN

Felt and Hessian Shop
34 Greville Street, London EC1
(wide-width)

FOAM

**Foamplan (Rubber and Plastics)
Co. Ltd.**
164 Holloway Road
London N7

PLASTIC GRANULES

Arrowtip Plastics Ltd.
31-35 Stannary Street,
London SE11
(for sag bag/large cushions)

UPHOLSTERY MATERIALS AND TOOLS

House of Foam Ltd
62-64 Hoe Street, Walthamstow,
London E17
(modern)

Russell Trading Co.
75 Paradise Street, Liverpool
(traditional)

Index

Acknowledgments

Title page: Gilles de Chabaneix; Page 6 John Heseltine; Page 8 John Heseltine; Page 10 Carey Tubb; Page 11 Timothy Beddow; Page 12 Guy Bouchet; Page 13 Collier Campbell; Page 14 John Heseltine; Page 16 John Heseltine; Page 18 Christine Hanscomb ; Page 19 Collier Campbell; Page 20 Gilles de Chabaneix; Page 21 Gilles de Chabaneix; Page 23 Collier Campbell; Page 24 Klaus G. Beyer; Page 25 Peo Eriksson (Sköma Hem) (top left), Christine Hanscomb (below right); Page 26 Christine Hanscomb ; Page 27 Collier Campbell (top right), John Vaughan (left); Page 28 John Heseltine; Page 29 Gilles de Chabaneix (top left), Ken Kirkwood (top right), Gilles de Chabaneix (bottom left), A. Sanderson & Son Ltd (bottom right); Page 30 David Burch; Page 31 David Burch; Page 32 *Homes and Gardens*, Syndications International (left), John Heseltine (middle); Page 33 David Burch; Page 34 Gilles de Chabaneix; Page 35 John Heseltine, Christine Hanscomb (bottom); Page 36 Ken Kirkwood; Page 37 John Heseltine, John Vaughan (inset); Page 38 Photographed by Ianthe Ruthven, room design by Gini Lavell, who specializes in hand-painted stencils; Page 39 John Heseltine, Collier Campbell (top inset), Souleiado (right inset); Page 40 *Homes and Gardens*, Syndications International; Page 41 John Heseltine, Collier Campbell (top inset), Gilles de Chabaneix (middle inset); Page 43 John Heseltine, *Homes and Gardens*, Syndications International (inset); Page 44 John Heseltine; Page 45 *Homes and Gardens*, Syndications International; Page 46 John Heseltine, Collier Campbell (inset); Page 47 Collier Campbell; Page 48 John Heseltine; Page 51 Gilles de Chabaneix; Page 53 Mary Fox Linton Ltd; Page 55 Christine Hanscomb ; Page 56 Gilles de Chabaneix; Page 59 Laura Ashley; Page 60 Gilles de Chabaneix; Page 62 Gilles de Chabaneix; Page 63 G P & J Baker Ltd; Page 65 Harrison Drape; Page 66 Laura Ashley; Page 68 Swish; Page 69 Véronique Lopez y Cabello; Page 71 Christine Hanscomb ; Page 73 Colour Counsellors; Page 74 Harrison Drape; Page 75 Crown Wallcoverings ('Kiss' range); Page 76 Harrison Drape; Page 77 John Heseltine; Page 79 Osborne & Little Ltd; Page 80 Interior Selection Ltd; Page 81 Laura Ashley (top), Osborne & Little Ltd (below); Page 82 John Heseltine; Page 83 Gilles de Chabaneix; Page 85 John Vaughan; Page 86 Mary Fox Linton Ltd; Page 88 Karen Bussolini (top), A. Sanderson & Sons Ltd (below); Page 91 Martex; Page 92 Syndications International; Page 93 ICI Dulux; Page 95 Christine Hanscomb ; Page 96 Osborne & Little Ltd; Page 97 Christine Hanscomb ; Page 98 Laura Ashley; Page 100 Gilles de Chabaneix; Page 101 Christine Hanscomb ; Page 104 ICI Dulux, 'Matchmaker' range (left), Gilles de Chabaneix (right); Page 105 Gilles de Chabaneix; Page 107 Asconti; Page 108 Interior Selection Ltd; Page 109 Laura Ashley; Page 110 Laura Ashley; Page 111 Karen Bussolini; Page 112 Gilles de Chabaneix; Page 113 Nobilis-Fontan; Page 114 Elizabeth Whiting and Associates; Page 115 John Heseltine; Page 116 Crown Wallcoverings ('Dash' range); Page 119 Mary Fox Linton Ltd; Page 121 Gilles de Chabaneix; Page 122 Gilles de Chabaneix; Page 123 John Heseltine; Page 124 Christine Hanscomb; Page 126 Photographed by Ianthe Ruthven, room design by Gini Lavell, who specializes in hand-painted stencils; Page 128 J P Stevens & Co Ltd; Page 130 Crown Wallcoverings ('Kiss' range) Page 131 Martex; Page 132 ICI Dulux ('Matchmaker' and 'Natural Whites' ranges); Page 133 ICI Dulux ('Matchmaker' and 'Natural Whites' ranges); Page 134 Laura Ashley; Page 135 Gilles de Chabaneix; Page 136 Colour Counsellors; Page 137 Gilles de Chabaneix; Page 138 Colour Counsellors; Page 139 Crown Wallcoverings ('Kiss' range); Page 140 Karen Bussolini; Page 141 Colefax and Fowler Designs Ltd; Page 143 Christine Hanscomb ; Page 144 Souleiado Ltd; Page 145 Christine Hanscomb ; Page 147 Christine Hanscomb ; Page 149 Elizabeth Whiting and Associates; Page 151 Harrison Drape; Page 152 G P Baker; Page 153 A. Sanderson & Sons Ltd.

The publishers wish to thank Wilkinson Sword Ltd and Fabritrak for their assistance.

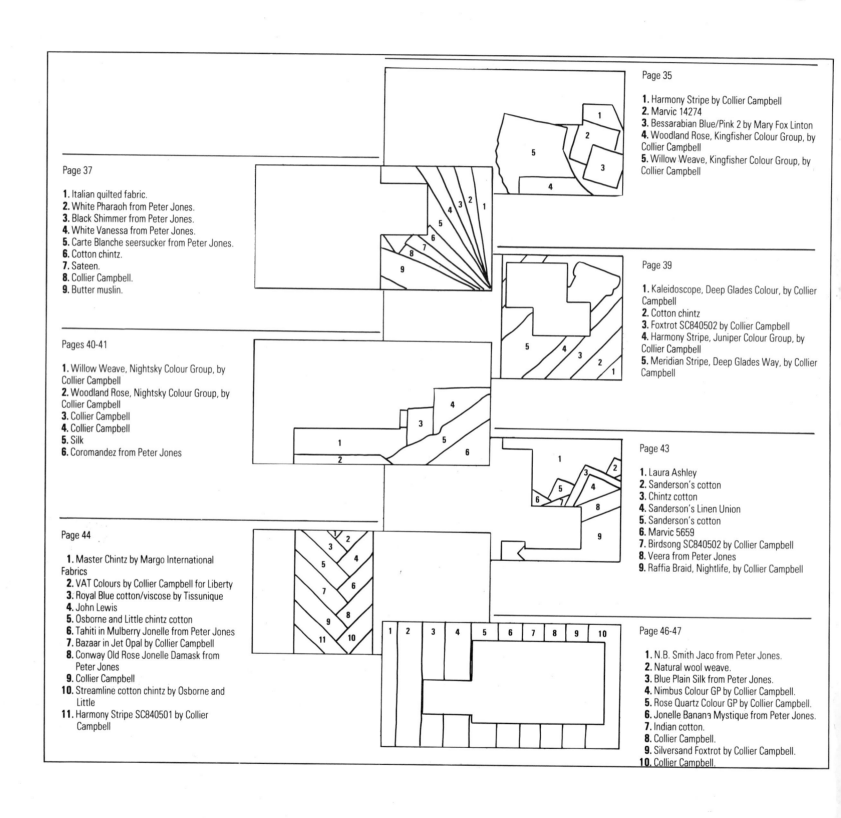

Page 35

1. Harmony Stripe by Collier Campbell
2. Marvic 14274
3. Bessarabian Blue/Pink 2 by Mary Fox Linton
4. Woodland Rose, Kingfisher Colour Group, by Collier Campbell
5. Willow Weave, Kingfisher Colour Group, by Collier Campbell

Page 37

1. Italian quilted fabric.
2. White Pharaoh from Peter Jones.
3. Black Shimmer from Peter Jones.
4. White Vanessa from Peter Jones.
5. Carte Blanche seersucker from Peter Jones.
6. Cotton chintz.
7. Sateen.
8. Collier Campbell.
9. Butter muslin.

Page 39

1. Kaleidoscope, Deep Glades Colour, by Collier Campbell
2. Cotton chintz
3. Foxtrot SC840502 by Collier Campbell
4. Harmony Stripe, Juniper Colour Group, by Collier Campbell
5. Meridian Stripe, Deep Glades Way, by Collier Campbell

Pages 40-41

1. Willow Weave, Nightsky Colour Group, by Collier Campbell
2. Woodland Rose, Nightsky Colour Group, by Collier Campbell
3. Collier Campbell
4. Collier Campbell
5. Silk
6. Coromandez from Peter Jones

Page 43

1. Laura Ashley
2. Sanderson's cotton
3. Chintz cotton
4. Sanderson's Linen Union
5. Sanderson's cotton
6. Marvic 5659
7. Birdsong SC840502 by Collier Campbell
8. Veera from Peter Jones
9. Raffia Braid, Nightlife, by Collier Campbell

Page 44

1. Master Chintz by Margo International Fabrics
2. VAT Colours by Collier Campbell for Liberty
3. Royal Blue cotton/viscose by Tissunique
4. John Lewis
5. Osborne and Little chintz cotton
6. Tahiti in Mulberry Jonelle from Peter Jones
7. Bazaar in Jet Opal by Collier Campbell
8. Conway Old Rose Jonelle Damask from Peter Jones
9. Collier Campbell
10. Streamline cotton chintz by Osborne and Little
11. Harmony Stripe SC840501 by Collier Campbell

Page 46-47

1. N.B. Smith Jaco from Peter Jones.
2. Natural wool weave.
3. Blue Plain Silk from Peter Jones.
4. Nimbus Colour GP by Collier Campbell.
5. Rose Quartz Colour GP by Collier Campbell.
6. Jonelle Banana Mystique from Peter Jones.
7. Indian cotton.
8. Collier Campbell.
9. Silversand Foxtrot by Collier Campbell.
10. Collier Campbell.